FRUITFUL
IN AFFLICTION

FRUITFUL IN AFFLICTION

JETAUNE RANDALL-SLAUGHTER

FRUITFUL IN AFFLICTION
Published by Purposely Created Publishing Group™
Copyright © 2018 Jetaune Randall-Slaughter

All rights reserved.

No part of this book may be reproduced, distributed or transmitted in any form by any means, graphic, electronic, or mechanical, including photocopy, recording, taping, or by any information storage or retrieval system, without permission in writing from the publisher, except in the case of reprints in the context of reviews, quotes, or references.

Unless otherwise indicated, scripture quotations are from the Holy Bible, King James Version. All rights reserved.

Scriptures marked NLT are taken from the New Living Translation®. Copyright © 1996, 2004, 2007, 2013 by Tyndale House Foundation. All rights reserved.

Scriptures marked NIV are taken from the New International Version®. Copyright © 1973, 1978, 1984, 2011 by Biblica, Inc.™. All rights reserved.

Printed in the United States of America
ISBN: 978-1-947054-89-9

Special discounts are available on bulk quantity purchases by book clubs, associations and special interest groups. For details email: sales@publishyourgift.com or call (888) 949-6228.

For information logon to:
www.PublishYourGift.com

DEDICATION

First, I would like to dedicate this book to my heavenly Father, my Lord and Savior— Jesus Christ, without whom I am ABSOLUTELY NOTHING; and the Holy Spirit for constantly teaching, educating, schooling, equipping, empowering, nudging, preparing, anointing, and comforting me throughout this entire process.

I would also like to recognize my husband and children, **Herbert Slaughter and Anthony & Bethany Wilson**, who have been a constant source of joy, humor, fun, love, and encouragement. You guys are my biggest cheerleaders!

To my sisters: **Janel Randall Patton and Jewel Mahan**. You were my FIRST FRIENDS, and we have been able to maintain an awesome covenant of love through Christ, as well as friendship. I appreciate you, **Janel** for your analytical, problem-solving, detail-oriented side. You are MY Olivia Pope! Your compassion and love for God's people encourages and amazes me. I love the worshipper you are and aspire to be like YOU. **Jewel**, you are my ride or die, secret service agent, health and beauty specialist, memory enhancement agent (you remember EVERYTHING) and all-around fun gal pal. It's comical when I think back to how much of a BRAT you were as a child, but I am THRILLED at the beautiful **JEWEL** of a woman of God you have BECOME! Keep striving and pressing to PLEASE HIM!

To the women who are not biological sisters, but my blood sisters through Jesus Christ, and have been a tremendous blessing in my life: **Sharrean (Shorn) McCrimmon, Jessica Beamer** (my spiritual "MOM" & mentor)**, Joanne Greer, Bridget McClerking, Shannan Eaddy, Renai Davis, Genova Clemons, Freda Holmes, Jacqui Williams, Evette Woolford, and countless others**. I appreciate your sisterhood, the times you listened, prayers and intercession sown, and the awesome wisdom I have received from you. I have gained so much love, support, and wisdom from you. I truly love and appreciate you.

To my parents: **Bill Randall, Janice Randall, and "Papa Joe" Ruff**. I've learned some awesome things from you guys. I'm glad God chose you, **Bill & Janice**, to be my parents. **"Papa Joe," thanks for teaching me, supporting me, and showing me a GREAT football team—the Dallas Cowboys! **Party, Baby!****

To my brothers: **Bill, Marc, Ravon, and Phil**. Thanks guys for always being there for me and supporting me.

To my new sister, **Joan T. Randall**, for the motivation and this awesome publisher who was the vehicle for getting this baby "birthed."

To my aunts: **Karen Johnson and Kathy Squalls**. I appreciate your love toward me and my family!

To my one and only Uncle Rudy. I love our Redskins and Cowboys football conversations. Plus, you're just the best uncle this side of Heaven. Love you so much!

To my cousins: **Khyyam, Trey** (rest in Heaven my brother/cousin/godbrother) and **Koda (Bear)**. Y'all are my brothers from another mother and I love y'all so much!

To my nephews and nieces: **Brianna, Stephen, Jade, Marc, Brandon, PJ, Kayla, Chelsea, Christina, and Justin**. Aunt Jetaune LOVES YOU ALL SO MUCH and prays that Christ would reign mightily in your lives and accomplish His purpose.

To Pastor Peyton Gray, First Lady Martha Gray, and the 4Him Covenant Church Family. Thanks for encouraging me in my gifting and talent, and for calling and praying me through. Thanks for being the awesome demonstration of the agape love of Christ in the earth. I appreciate you.

To my Intercessory Sisters: Ganella, Nicole, Lydia, Christina, Kenyetta, Lisa, Paula, and CeCe. Y'all know how to bombard Heaven on my behalf and I'm ever so grateful!

To Diahanna Stevens for pushing and encouraging me to keep writing when I was experiencing writer's block and just plain feeling like I'd never be able to get it done. Your prayers and intercession mean the world to me. Thanks so much!

TABLE OF CONTENTS

Introduction 1

CHAPTER 1:
I Never Fit In 3

CHAPTER 2:
My Mouth: The Mess and the Message 15

CHAPTER 3:
Working the Word with Your Words 19

CHAPTER 4:
Weight Loss: God's Way 33

CHAPTER 5:
Praise & Worship: Necessary Weapons 41

CHAPTER 6:
Dealing with Divorce 49

CHAPTER 7:
Dealing with Rejection, Loneliness, and Being
Misunderstood 57

CHAPTER 8:
Dealing with the Battle Between My Ears (My Mind) ... 69

CHAPTER 9:
Overcoming Barrenness 77

CHAPTER 10:
Letting It Go! Overcoming Unforgiveness 81

CHAPTER 11:
The Manifestation Is Finally Here! 91

About the Author 99

INTRODUCTION

Writing a book is very difficult because even though you know what you want to say getting started is hard. It is my desire that through this book you will find increased peace, praise, power, and purpose, despite the rough trials and tribulations you are currently enduring.

CHAPTER 1

I NEVER FIT IN

Looking at my life, I have never been a person who fit in. I was the surprise baby who was sickly, colicky, and had more ear infections than you can shake a stick at. I was the chubby, overfed baby who always cried and couldn't be soothed. I was a late walker (almost 16 months old). As much as I LOVE PEOPLE—being around them, talking, laughing, and having fun, etc., I often feel like a stranger or that something is wrong with me. I was often asked, "Are you adopted?" (even though I was the OLDEST CHILD). I was a skinny, tall kid with an "apple head." As a result, I felt awkward, ugly, and out of place. Now, with a slightly larger figure, I still frequently feel like the proverbial square peg trying to fit into the round hole. Then, the light bulb from the Word of God WENT OFF like a FOUR-ALARM FIRE in my head! The Lord sweetly reminded me that "I am fearfully and wonderfully made" (Psalm 139:14, NIV). Though I was conceived in an illegal, unauthorized, and unbiblical circumstance, I was predestined in the mind of

God. I may be strange looking and strange acting (at times), nevertheless, I am part of a divine purpose. It doesn't have to be understood to be correct. You shouldn't feel bad because you don't fit in. Did you ever stop to think that you fitting in wasn't God's intention? The things that make you YOU are the very things that the Lord will use to bring glory to Himself and draw others to His Son, Jesus. Stop worrying about whether you are too tall, too dark, too light, too fat, too skinny, or if your hair is too nappy, too straight, or too curly and embrace the individuality to which you are assigned on this earth. It is a slap in the Lord's face to be SOMETHING YOU'RE NOT! You have heard it said many times before: "This world would be boring if everyone was the same, looked the same, and acted the same." Well, my friend, that applies to YOU!

Let's say for a minute that you have been acting in a manner outside of the way you were created. Know this, you can BEGIN AGAIN. You're probably wondering, "How in the Sam Hill do I DO THAT?" It won't be easy because you have to UNLEARN some behaviors, some thought patterns, and some word curses that were spoken over your life as a child. This is going to be a PROCESS and not an overnight occurrence. Start with knowing your VALUE. Pennies in and of themselves don't look very valuable, until you check the date. Those are usually the ones that are worn, dirty looking, and old. Those are the ones that, when polished, you see how much they are really worth. The same thing applies to you. You may have been through some serious mess! Some of you may have endured verbal, physical, mental, and even sexual abuse. Some of you grew up in a seemingly perfect two-parent household, but felt ugly, misunderstood, alone, rejected, were constantly being compared to other family members, etc. This doesn't have to be YOUR LOT! You may have been overlooked, even left for dead, but it doesn't change God's plan or mind concerning YOU! When I reflect on my life, although I was the firstborn daughter, granddaughter, goddaughter, great-granddaughter, niece, cousin, and sister, I felt rejected many times and was often treated as an inconvenience of my parents' youthful indiscretion. A great point of reference I had was in Ezekiel 16:4. It refers to someone who was pretty much like babies in news stories who are put in a cardboard box or dumpster when born and left to fend for themselves. This child wasn't even given the luxury of being bathed! The umbilical cord wasn't even cut! How CRUEL is that? They weren't wanted from the OUTSET! No one salted them. Salting was a Jewish custom in which the midwife would add salt to the water after a baby was born to remove the amniotic fluid and blood, and to prevent the skin from receiving rashes, etc. It was a purification process to get you ready for the world in which you would be living. Now, push PAUSE, I have a question for you. How many times did you need someone to help cleanse you and prepare you for life, yet you were just left to yourself? It almost doesn't seem fair. No one covered or clothed you. Man, that's rough! No one took any interest in you. You were an afterthought. With that type of introduction into this (already cruel) world, it could push you to attempt suicide. However, you must keep in mind that you would be trying to UNDO the very purpose for which you are HERE! Look at ALL that you have endured. Some people have died for LESS! You are on this side of the dirt! You are BLESSED! You have so much to thank and praise God for! Tragedy is your stepping stone! Pain is your catapult to promise! You must look past your past to endure your present and embrace your promise. Alas, I digress. Ezekiel 16:6 indicates that the Lord saw the condition of this child, but He did something awesome. Even before He did anything PHYSICAL… He said LIVE! God has already SPOKEN LIFE to you, even if you don't see it! I thought of another example. I don't by any means have a green thumb, but it made me think of those folks who have a plant that is dying and they (in an effort to keep the plant alive and ensure that it thrives) speak to it on a regular basis. They are not moved by the externals of what has NOT happened with the plant (lack of moisture, growth, sun, etc.), they just keep making sure that they FEED the plant with water, good food, and sunlight. Take special note of that: they feed the plant water. So, if you're trying to get purified, you are going to have to activate the same principles. Quench your spirit man with the Water (the Holy Spirit). Start by yielding your spirit to the Holy Spirit. He is your Teacher and He will lead and guide you into all truth (John 14:17). He will reveal more of Christ's nature, character, and love to us (John 14:22). He is God's representative and advocate for us and IN us. He will remind us of everything Jesus taught the disciples (John 14:26, John 15:26-27). He will comfort you and bring you peace (John 14:1, Isaiah 26:3). He will show you how to respond to adverse circumstances. He will give you discernment and let you know when something just ain't RIGHT. He will empower you to be obedient to the Word of God. He will warn you of any temptations that would hinder you in your walk with Christ, AND provide a way of escape (1 Corinthians 10:13). Interestingly enough, nothing other than His presence will satisfy your thirst. It's like knowing you're REALLY THIRSTY, but instead of reaching for water, you reach for a soda, which is a temporary fix. You will have all the energy, sugar, carbs, and flavor, but soon thereafter, you're thirsty again. Next, you will need to feed your spirit with good spiritual food. You will need a daily (and sometimes more than that) diet of the Word of God. It's not enough to have a short devotional or read a quick Bible verse, you're going to need to ingest, digest, and regurgitate the Word of God in order to grow. If this is a new walk with the Lord, you will have to start with small doses (like 15 minutes or a Bible devotional), but as you continue to feed yourself with the Word, you're going to want more and more of it. This will come with regular Bible Study at your local Bible-teaching assembly or fellowship. Just like in the beginning of a child's life, they crave milk. As they grow and develop, their appetite increases for more solid food, and ultimately tougher meat (1 Peter 2:2). As a baby, you basically only have your parents feeding you. They will provide you with all the nourishment you need. Spiritually so, the Lord will provide a pastor who will feed you God's Word. If they are a true man or woman of God, what they give you will benefit your life, and provide wisdom and balance so that you can be a productive citizen in God's kingdom and in the world. Also, as you grow in your walk with Christ, you will learn that you can't eat from everybody's table. Just like you wouldn't go to each of your neighbor's houses for their mac and cheese because you know how GOOD your mother's is, you will also learn, through time, that some things will not agree with your spiritual palate. Some things simply don't apply to you. There won't be anything that will satisfy you quite like the Word! You will also find that when you miss time in the Word, you will start to feel out of sorts. Don't worry, just pick up where you left off, and you will find cohesiveness being restored in your walk with God. Backsliding doesn't happen overnight (that's something I will address in another chapter)! Been there, done that! The Word will provide comfort, truth, freedom, power, and strength. It is most definitely a weapon in your arsenal that you will find you can't do without! (1 Peter 1:25, Psalm 119:114, Job 23:12, Psalm 19, Psalm 119:9-11, Psalm 119:16-17). Thirdly, you will need light in order to grow. The spiritual light is not just the Word of God (Psalm 119:105), but the very presence of God Himself. You will need to spend time in His presence through prayer, praise, thanksgiving, and worship. The awesome thing about light is that it eradicates DARKNESS and reveals what is actually going on!

Jesus will do that for ya! There were times when I have been exhausted and sleepy, but I knew I needed to wake my happy tail up to pray. And once I got into the presence of the King, the Almighty God, my Prince of Peace, it's amazing how alert I became. I also discovered that the questions I presented to Him during prayer were answered and confirmed during the course of my day. Even if there wasn't an immediate answer, I went away KNOWING THERE WOULD BE! It's also amazing how peaceful my day goes or even how I handle adversity. My prayer life is similar to a romantic relationship, but even MORE intimate. What I mean is, the more time I spend with the Lord, the MORE I want to be with and PLEASE Him! What started out as a CHORE had in essence become a SWEET DELIGHT! (Psalm 16:11). It went from the task I was taught at Bible Study and Sunday School to an absolute JOY and NECESSITY. My body now awakens around that time, just to be with Him. Guess what? I learned that my prayer life is not about me spouting off my To Do List for God, but it has become a loving and intimate relationship with my Father. And as I learn more about Him and how to become a DOER of all He says, there is such an indescribable peace and favor that surrounds my life. He is my everything! Part of dwelling in His light comes through the vehicle of praise and worship. For those of us who have endured much hurt, abuse, and rejection, that may sound like a foreign concept, especially if you've poured your heart into people who don't return the love. This may have been from a father, mother, boyfriend, girlfriend, relative, or friend. Since we are made in the image and likeness of God, we possess His nature and affinity to give and receive praise. You ever notice that when someone tells us how nice we look, we BLUSH or SMILE (almost like Celie did on *The Color Purple* when Shug Avery told her she had a pretty smile. LOL!)? Well, when you tell God how WONDERFUL, MIGHTY, FAITHFUL, LOVING, GRACIOUS, MERCIFUL, etc., He is… it makes His Heart SMILE! Let me give you this warning though, He can tell if you are just saying it because you WANT SOMETHING (like kids are known to do) or if you are SINCERE with your praise. You can't fake the funk with Him, so don't even TRY IT! Start with saying, "Thank you, Lord, for (fill in the blanks)," and as that increases start praising Him for (fill in the blanks), and then you will progressively move to worship which is SIMPLY because He's GOD! That's total ADORATION! I notice that there are times when I just want to be with my husband, not because I want him to do anything, but just to spend time with him. Words aren't even involved. There are times when we will be on the phone with each other and there isn't a lot of talking. It's sometimes just listening to each other breathing. There's just a sweetness about his presence that I live for. That didn't just HAPPEN. It evolved through spending regular time with him. When we started dating, it progressed from the interests we both shared, to the things we disliked or liked, to wanting to make each other happy. Your relationship with God will be similar. You will become acquainted with Him, then you will discover (through His Word) the things that displease Him, and consequently, you will find out the things that make Him happy. You will find that making Him happy (done through your obedience) will be your life's quest.

Returning to the green thumb analogy, I want to encourage you to SPEAK to YOURSELF that things in your LIFE will change and turn around. You most assuredly will see awesome results. You have the things you have and do the things you do because of WORDS and the way you think. Hmm! Words fashion and shape things into existence. The earth was formed by the words uttered out of the mouth of God (Genesis 1:3, 1:5-12). So, don't buy into the lie, "Sticks and stones may break my bones, but words will never hurt me." If that was the case, nothing hurtful or abusive that people said would've affected us. Curse words are not just the four, five, and twelve letter expletives we hear on television shows, see in movies, or read about in magazines or blogs. They were words that were not only spoken to us, but to our parents and ancestors. It has been a struggle for me to live down things because of some of the word curses that were spoken over me. What word curses were spoken over you? They might have started out like, "You're stupid," "You're ugly," "You'll never amount to anything," "You'll never have anything," "You're always gonna (fill in the blank)," "You're just like your mamma, daddy, uncle, or auntie." I'm so thankful the Word of God, not the words of man, can dictate the future of my life! (Jeremiah 29:11). No matter how many years or how many word curses were spoken over you, you can make the conscious decision THIS DAY to reverse the curse by the words of your mouth. However, you will have to start by renewing your mind with the Word of God. The following verses will need to be written down on index cards, memorized, and meditated upon (chew on them over and over daily) in order to achieve victory over the enemy. Remember Jesus addressed the enemy (the devil, Satan) by using the Word of God. He always started by saying, "It is written…"

Let's look at some verses that will help you.

Proverbs 18:21 (KJV)—"Death and life are in the power of the tongue: and they that love it shall eat the fruit thereof."

Matthew 4:4 (KJV)—"But he answered and said, It is written, Man shall not live by bread alone, but by every word that proceedeth out of the mouth of God."

Psalm 139:13-14 (KJV)—"For thou hast possessed my reins: thou hast covered me in my mother's womb. I will praise thee; for I am fearfully and wonderfully made: marvellous are thy works; and that my soul knoweth right well."

Psalm 119:105 (KJV)—"Thy word *is* a lamp unto my feet, and a light unto my path."

Luke 18:1 (KJV)—"And he spake a parable unto them *to this end*, that men ought always to pray, and not to faint;"

Ephesians 6:10-18 (KJV)—"Finally, my brethren, be strong in the Lord, and in the power of his might. Put on the whole armour of God, that ye may be able to stand against the wiles of the devil. For we wrestle not against flesh and blood, but against principalities, against powers, against the rulers of the darkness of this world, against spiritual wickedness in high *places*. Wherefore take unto you the whole armour of God, that ye may be able to withstand in the evil day, and having done all, to stand. Stand therefore, having your loins girt about with truth, and having on the breastplate of righteousness; And your feet shod with the preparation of the gospel of peace; Above all, taking the shield of faith, wherewith ye shall be able to quench all the fiery darts of the wicked. And take the helmet of salvation, and the sword of the Spirit, which is the word of God: Praying always with all prayer and supplication in the Spirit, and watching thereunto with all perseverance and supplication for all saints;"

Mark 11:22-24-22 (KJV)—"And Jesus answering saith unto them, Have faith in God. For verily I say unto you, That whosoever shall say unto this mountain, Be thou removed, and be thou cast into the sea; and shall not doubt in his heart, but shall believe that those things which he saith shall come to pass; he shall have whatsoever he saith. Therefore, I say unto you, What things soever ye desire, when ye pray, believe that ye receive *them*, and ye shall have *them*."

Isaiah 54:17 (KJV)—"No weapon that is formed against thee shall prosper; and every tongue *that* shall rise against thee in judgment thou shalt condemn. This *is* the heritage of the servants of the LORD, and their righteousness *is* of me, saith the LORD."

Of course, there are a plethora of Scriptures, but these will be the ones that will help you immediately.

CHAPTER 2

MY MOUTH: THE MESS AND THE MESSAGE

One of the things about me that people probably can say is that I don't ever have a problem TALKING. I was an early talker as a baby and would just chatter away! As I grew older, it became obvious that I was a VERY, VERY, VERY DIRECT and OUTSPOKEN child, almost to a fault! It's the prophet in me! One incident I recall is when I was about three years old. My father had his boss over for dinner, and he kept prodding me to "Sing for the man, Jetaune." And as most little kids do when they are prodded to PERFORM, they RESIST it with a passion. I resisted for a few minutes, but then I decided to give in to my father's ANNOYING demand. Before we go any further with this story, know that my father's supervisor was a white Caucasian male. Anywho, I decided to sing a song by Sly and the Family Stone that has a very negative term that is not very kind to use with not only my ethnicity but others as well. Needless to say, after that musical rendition, my father didn't ask me to do anymore singing for company that came to the house. That was one of the infallible proofs that I had QUITE THE MOUTH on me. While I was never a person who used much profanity, even after my new life in Christ, the very thing God wanted to use was at times my Achilles Heel! I would often be guilty of talking too much at the wrong time, to the wrong person, about the wrong thing. I can quite honestly say, I've been guilty of being the gossiper, talebearer, tattletale, and in some instances, the liar. Little did I know, those things would become the very catalyst for my spiritual education.

One of things I learned was, "Everything that comes to your mind doesn't need to be said or repeated!" Self-control must be employed and active. You may be presented with some interesting information about someone or even a compelling circumstance, that is when you have been given a divine opportunity to PRAY. Can you be TRUSTED with someone's personal and confidential information? Are you a person of integrity? I know it's appealing, interesting, and exciting, but can you HOLD YOUR TONGUE? You must be trained by the Holy Spirit so that you walk in discretion and honor. You most certainly do NOT want to be a person who has a diarrhea mouth or a bad refrigerator mouth (one that can't keep ANYTHING).

The majority of my giftings (spiritually, and in some instances naturally) are in my MOUTH. Everything from singing (I can hold a tune, but I am not a CeCe Winans or Yolanda Adams), to encouraging, preaching, teaching, and even making people laugh with my wit and humor. It is not my intention to come across as arrogant, I am just stressing my strengths.

It is also a fact that I have not always been the wisest person when using this gifted and anointed mouth. I've said things out of season, to the wrong person, and with the wrong attitude and spirit. If that's you and you can truly comprehend where I'm coming from, here are some Scriptures upon which you can meditate:

Job 6:24 (KJV): "Teach me, and I will hold my tongue: and cause me to understand wherein I have erred."

Job 8:2 (KJV): "How long wilt thou speak these things? and how long shall the words of thy mouth be like a strong wind?"

Proverbs 6:2 (KJV): "Thou art snared with the words of thy mouth, thou art taken with the words of thy mouth."

Proverbs 18:21 (KJV): "Death and life are in the power of the tongue: and they that love it shall eat the fruit thereof."

Psalms 19:14 (KJV): "Let the words of my mouth, and the meditation of my heart, be acceptable in thy sight, O LORD, my strength, and my redeemer."

Child of God, you must understand that as a believer your mouth contains a MESSAGE. The message not only includes the Gospel of Jesus Christ, but the way God has gifted and blessed you to overcome GREAT ADVERSITY is in your TESTIMONY. Remember the Word of the Lord that reads in Revelation 12:11 (KJV), "And they overcame him by the blood of the Lamb, and by the word of their testimony; and they loved not their lives unto the death." What you have endured, gone through, and suffered is NOT FOR YOU. It is the vehicle by which God is getting the glory. It is to edify and build up others. It is for their encouragement and strength.

What have you been doing with your mouth during this season of adversity and testing? We will delve more into that in the next chapter, as it can be quite extensive.

CHAPTER 3

WORKING THE WORD WITH YOUR WORDS

As previously discussed in chapter two, your mouth contains a MESSAGE, even if at times it was an inevitable MESS! Looking back over my life, if I could take back some of the things I said, WHY I said them, and HOW I said them, I definitely would. Nevertheless, I'm forgetting things which are behind me and reaching to those things which are before me. I do, indeed, press toward the mark of the prize of the high calling of God in Christ Jesus. It's going to take a conscious effort to do this. What you do with your mouth in this (or any other) season is KEY. First, and foremost, you need to evaluate and examine what you've been doing. When problems, obstacles, trials, or afflictions come, what is the FIRST THING you do? Cry? Cuss? Curse? Gossip? Complain? Whine? Moan? Murmur? Do you instantaneously pray? Praise? Worship? Confess? Declare? Decree? No matter what it is, it needs to be PRODUCTIVE! The one thing (among many things) that Jesus did that I truly admired is Jesus NEVER WASTED HIS WORDS. He never engaged in arguments, debates, etc. He simply SPOKE THE WORD. Not only did He SPEAK THE WORD, but He was wise in both the authority and season in which He spoke. You can be 100 percent correct with the truthfulness of the Word God has put in your mouth, however, if it's out of season, it can cause damage. Can you imagine trying to get a fresh, ripe watermelon in November? If you managed to get it, it would cost you more. "Why is that?" you might ask. Because it isn't the season for watermelon. The winter and fall seasons consist of apples, bananas, grapes, oranges, pumpkins, squash, zucchini, potatoes, etc. The summer season is the one for watermelons, strawberries, etc. You don't want to be found guilty of saying the RIGHT THING at the WRONG TIME. For example, the Lord may show you someone is being PROMOTED, and they have been going through great tribulation and testing. Is it your job to tell them RIGHT AWAY they are being promoted? NOT NECESSARILY. The reason the Lord entrusted you with the information first is so that you would PRAY. What are you praying for? You are praying for the Lord to PREPARE them for their promotion. He is ALWAYS working on our character so that we walk in integrity and grace. To everything there is a season. Ecclesiastes 3:1-8 (KJV) records, "To every thing there is a season, and a time to every purpose under the heaven: A time to be born, and a time to die; a time to plant, and a time to pluck up that which is planted; A time to kill, and a time to heal; a time to break down, and a time to build up; A time to weep, and a time to laugh; a time to mourn, and a time to dance; A time to cast away stones, and a time to gather stones together; a time to embrace, and a time to refrain from embracing; A time to get, and a time to lose; a time to keep, and a time to cast away; A time to rend, and a time to sew; a time to keep silence, and a time to speak; A time to love, and a time to hate; a time of war, and a time of peace."

The question to you my dear brother and sister is, what words are you sowing in this season? In the words of Dr. Phil, "How's that working for you?" Is what you are saying HELPING your life, ADDING to your life, or DESTROYING everything around you? Are the words you are speaking drawing you closer to Christ or pushing you further and further away? I have never seen so many "Carnal Christians"! What do I mean by that? Well, what I mean is that instead of letting the Holy Spirit govern their emotions, circumstances, and flesh, they are choosing to allow their emotions to govern their actions. Among these manifestations are: cussing, fussing, gossiping, murmuring, complaining, whining, getting and staying offended, being super-sensitive, and moving in and yielding to unforgiveness, bitterness, and resentment, just to name a few. Not only that, we are very familiar with church-lingo, catch-phrases, traditions, and the things we do in church, but when it comes to being led by the Holy Spirit in our everyday life, we fall short with our responses. We are far too distracted by any and everything. TVs, iPads, computers, and cell phones, just to name a few, have taken over our lives. Books being held in our hands are a rarity these days. (Let me say, I'm not against any of these items. I am just indicating how we're technologically savvy, but spiritually depraved and anemic.) We don't know the Word (not just memorizing and quoting, but WALKING IT OUT) as we should. In a time where social media is the norm, our brothers and sisters in Christ fall prey to the postings of Facebook friends and Twitter and Instagram followers who aren't discriminatory with their words. They don't care about what they say; they just want to "put it all out there." They allow the tiniest opinion, comment, or statement to bother them. They don't seem to recognize their God-given authority. Had they known or embraced this heavenly authority, they wouldn't allow things to consume or bother them as much. That's not to say that we are ROBOTS and we have NO EMOTIONS, it's just that we choose what we allow to bother us! You must learn to pick your battles. Know this, the battle the Lord allows you to engage in will be one where you can be VICTORIOUS!

Let's take a moment and see how we can **Work the Word with our Words**. Turn to Ephesians 6:10 (KJV): "Finally, my brethren, be strong in the Lord, and in the power of his might." We must first recognize what we've been given, and that's STRENGTH. The Scripture says to BE STRONG… not TRY to Be Strong or I WISH I was strong. The Lord is well aware that in and of yourself, you don't have the ability to overcome adverse circumstances, that's why He refers to this two-fold spiritual dynamic duo. Your strength will be "in the Lord" and in the power of "his might." According to Vine's Expository Dictionary, the following definitions apply for both the terms "strong in the Lord" and "power of his might."

"Strong in the Lord"

Enable:

"to render strong" (*dunamis*, "power"), is translated "enabled" in 1 Timothy 1:12, "inwardly strengthened," suggesting strength in soul and purpose (Philippians 4:13).

"Power of His might"

Dominion (have… over):

"force, strength, might," more especially "manifested power," is derived from a root *kra—*, "to perfect, to complete:" "creator" is probably connected. It also signifies "dominion," and is so rendered frequently in doxologies.

Note: Synonymous words are *bia*, "force," often oppressive, *dunamis*, "power," especially "inherent power;" *energeia*, "power" especially in exercise, operative power.

In a nutshell, you've been given a divine enablement to stand against the enemy. It is with His power and might that you can do awesome things to terrorize, annihilate, and destroy the works of the enemy's kingdom. You were DEPU-

TIZED, even better than Barney Fife (from *The Andy Griffith Show*) who was given one bullet, but not the permission to use it. Your authority was not only manifested physically, but delegated from Heaven! What a blessing! It's amazing how so many people want to operate under the power of God, but haven't been given permission to do so. For example, the seven sons of Sceva (Acts 19:14-16). They wanted to utilize this anointing, this power, but couldn't. This was probably because one was the son of a religious leader, so he was familiar with religious dogma, doctrine, etc.; however, he wasn't connected to the Spirit of the living God! Also, Sceva was another word for mind reader, meaning he was probably involved with occultism and pagan activities. There is no way the Lord will utilize you to accomplish His purpose if you work for the other team.

The next function we must be fully engaged in on a consistent and daily basis is **Putting on the Whole Armor of God**! This involves IMMEDIATE ACTION. Just as you put on your clothes every day after showering, you must do the same thing spiritually. God is not just going to drop power out of the sky so you can defeat the enemy. This is a proactive, joint venture between YOU and the Holy Spirit. The Greek word for put is enduo, from which we get the word endue. It's like when you sink into your clothing, indicating an easy transition from nakedness to being clothed. The adjustment is definitely EASIER when the Holy Spirit is the teacher. As I stated previously, it's much more difficult, and oftentimes futile, if you have to do it by yourself. Your greatest efforts fail in comparison to what the Holy Spirit can do THROUGH you.

Let's look at our verse, Ephesians 6:11 (KJV), again. "Put on the whole armour of God, that ye may be able to stand against the wiles of the devil." Now, having said that, WHAT you put on is just as important as the action involved. You are now about to sink yourself into some serious WMD (Weapons of Mass Destruction). These weapons are going to be the very weapons that are more offensive than defensive, but are equally as powerful nonetheless. Think about this for a minute, you are given not only heavenly authority, but spiritual weaponry to literally handle demons of all sizes, shapes, and colors. I remember an old praying deacon I used to go to church with would say, "God don't put no LOLLIPOPS in no TOOLBOX!" In other words, whatever you need will be the right equipment to handle the job.

You don't go to war fighting with a squirt gun. The whole armor of God is SERIOUS BUSINESS. You aren't given a piece here and a piece there. You are given the whole kit and caboodle. For example, when you go into the army, you are given a certain amount of underwear, boots, shirts, shorts, caps, cold weather gear and black gloves, just to name a few things. However, you are not given things for personal hygiene, and weapons for combat are given after a certain amount of training.

The next thing you should be mindful of is that your armor has a distinct PURPOSE. That purpose is to stand against the wiles of the devil. "What are wiles?" you may ask. Vine's Expository Dictionary defines it as follows. **Wiles:** *methodia or –eia* denotes "craft, deceit" (*meta*, "after," *hodos*, "a way"). "a cunning device, a wile," and is translated "wiles (of error)" in Ephesians 4:14, RV [AV paraphrases it, "they lie in wait (to deceive)"], lit., "(with a view to) the craft (singular) of deceit;" in Ephesians 6:11, "the wiles (plural) (of the Devil.)" Your weapons are going to assist you in gaining victory over the strategies and cunning tactics of the enemy. That is SO POWERFUL.

One of the biggest battles we contend with is NOT that we fight, but WHO we fight. "For we wrestle not against flesh and blood [people and what they do], but against principalities, against powers, against the rulers of the darkness of this world, against spiritual wickedness in high *places*" (Ephesians 6:12). So often when we are going through our battles, tests, trials, tribulations, obstacles, etc., we tend to look at the people involved as our enemies. They very WELL may be the people the enemy is using; however, it's NOT THEM, but the spirit of the enemy that's operating in them. We must look beyond their actions, attitudes, and behavior. Now, let's break this verse down a little further. Let's start with "against principalities." What exactly ARE principalities? It's the Greek word arche (pronounced ar-KAY). The Vine's Expository Dictionary defines it as: **Begin, Beginning, Beginner**; "a beginning."

The root *arch* primarily indicated what was of worth. Hence the verb *archo* meant "to be first," and *archon* denoted "a ruler." Another description by the Vine's Expository Dictionary is **Principality**: "beginning, government, rule," is used of supramundane beings who exercise rule, called "principalities;"

1. the person or thing that commences, the first person or thing in a series, the leader.

2. that by which anything begins to be, the origin, the active cause.

3. the extremity of a thing; of the corners of a sail.

4. the first place, principality, rule, magistracy, of angels and demons.

This would be the head demon or head spirit; "The Big Man on Campus." Next, we will define the term "against powers." Powers are defined in a myriad of ways. The Greek word is exousia (EX-OO-SEE-AHH). According to Vine's Expository Dictionary, it means **Authority:**

1. denotes "authority" (from the impersonal verb *exesti,* "it is lawful"). From the meaning of "leave or permission," or liberty of doing as one pleases; physical and mental power.

   1a. the ability or strength with which one is endued, which he either possesses or exercises

2. the power of authority (influence) and of right (privilege)

3. the power of rule or government (the power of him whose will and commands must be submitted to by others and obeyed)

These spirits are people (I'm using that term loosely) with demonic authority and jurisdiction. They have been given satanic access to terrorize and invoke wickedness.

Moving on to "against the rulers of the darkness of this world." Rulers is defined, both in the Strong's Concordance and Vine's Dictionary, as kosmokrator. It is not a literal or physical ruler, but as I previously stated, it's somebody satanically appointed to walk in darkness, evil intent, and activity. They just happen to utilize human bodies.

The whole armor of God is so vitally important that Apostle Paul mentioned it again in Ephesians 6:13 (NJV). Except this time he said, "TAKE UNTO YOU THE WHOLE ARMOUR OF God." Hmm, there's a distinct difference between putting on the armor of God and taking unto you the armor of God. When you put on the armor of God, it's just like when you are dressing yourself. When the Scripture references the verse by saying "take unto you," it is personal. You not only physically lift the weapons that Heaven has blessed and anointed you to use, but it's personal because you can use each weapon as it applies to your personal dilemma or circumstance. As you utilize your weaponry in faith, you become a skilled soldier in battle and warfare! Trust and believe, life will offer you plenty of opportunities to practice. Between the battle with bills, children, job, school, family, ministry, health (illness), and a myriad of life's issues, you can become armed and dangerous to the kingdom of darkness. You will be a serious threat and terrorize the hosts of hell!

The interesting thing about me (most of my family and friends know this) is that I am NOT a fighter. I literally have to be PUSHED into confrontation before I address things. It reminds me of when I was in junior high school, and there was this girl who falsely accused me of talking about her. Mind you, I didn't know the girl from a can of paint. While in the cafeteria at lunch, she approached me, pushed me, then hit me. Finally, I got a revelation—I can't keep allowing this girl to hit me. So, I struck back. After wind-milling a few random and sporadic punches, some scratching and scrapping, oddly enough, I won the fight! What you need to understand about this girl is that she was in the 9th grade for about three years, she was bigger and heavier than the average teenage girl, and she had a voice like Barry White. Comically, her taller, but younger sister who had an even DEEPER voice was THRILLED I beat up her sister! Wasn't that a hoot? However, the sad part was that even though I defeated my enemy, my bully, I became a slave to her out of fear. It started when she had me doing her homework every day. My mom would wonder why it took me so long to complete my homework. She also had me cheating on tests to help her out. One day, when I was walking her home from school, I saw my mother's car parked in front of her apartment. I thought, "OMG! What is she doing HERE?" As we went into her house, her mother approached her about what she had been doing to me, and proceeded to whip her behind RIGHT IN FRONT OF ME!

There are several spiritual lessons I took from my experiences with that young lady: 1) The Lord used what I had in me to enable me to defeat my enemy ("Greater is he that is in you, than he that is in the world—1 John 4:4, KJV). 2) I don't need to allow fear or intimidation to control me for any length of time. 3) God, as your Father, will fight for you and allow you to see your enemies defeated right before your eyes.

When we first gave our lives to Christ (got saved), errant pastors, preachers, and Bible teachers told us that there would be no problems. However, that is contrary to what the Bible teaches. They falsely presented "the pie in the sky" and "the great by and by" messages, and it FLOORED US when things didn't go as planned. It's not whether you will be in warfare or not, because as a believer you most assuredly are AUTOMATICALLY ENROLLED in it. Jesus himself revealed in John 16:33 (KJV), "These things I have spoken unto you, that in me ye might have peace. In the world ye shall have tribulation: but be of good cheer; I have overcome the world."

It's not that we WON'T go through things (tests, trials, temptations, troubles, etc.), but rather, HOW WE GO THROUGH. The instruction was given by Jesus to BE OF

GOOD CHEER! In essence, CHEER UP! Why? Because He (referring to Jesus) has OVERCOME the world. He has ACHIEVED VICTORY over the world's system, their plots, their plans, their schemes, their ploys, and their conspiracies. So then, since Jesus now resides in us as a result of personal salvation, that same victory belongs to us! He achieved it when He shed His precious blood on the cross for us. You don't have to allow your circumstances to rule over you. You can indeed RULE OVER THEM!

CHAPTER 4

WEIGHT LOSS: GOD'S WAY

This chapter seems like such a far cry from the previous chapter; however, there is definitely a connection and divine thread, given by the Holy Spirit who is our teacher and biggest cheerleader.

Although I was a chubby baby (as discussed in the first chapter), I didn't struggle much with my weight until my late teens and adult years. I distinctly remember that I weighed in at 139 pounds at age 17, and my mom said, "You need to watch it because you're putting on weight." Looking at that number now is such a joke because I'm more than double that weight at age 51. After attending a church that firmly believed in prayer and fasting, I lost a lot of weight. (I have since marriage, childbirth, and life's issues regained that lost weight and even more.) Even though my cholesterol levels and blood pressure are fantastic, the fact remains that if I don't lose weight, several health risks will be my downfall. They include: heart attack, heart disease, stroke, diabetes, breathing and respiratory issues, sleep apnea, poor circulation, back, knee, joint problems, and countless other health issues. Not to mention there are emotional factors that come into play—you don't feel as beautiful and you're more self-conscious of people critiquing your appearance, abilities, etc. Even though I pretty much possess an adequate view of my physical person, beauty, etc., I'm self-conscious about my double-chin, shape, and certain physical attributes I feel would not be an issue if I were thinner. Suffice it to say, there are thinner women who don't feel beautiful, no matter how small they get. That's how eating disorders like bulimia and anorexia develop.

In a nutshell, and I know I'll get varying opinions and responses on this, being OVERWEIGHT or OBESE is just not good for ANYONE, no matter your ethnicity, skin color, height, or age. The same principle applies to you SPIRITUALLY. Let's digress for a minute and look at how weight gain itself occurs. Some of it can develop from genetic pre-disposition, environment, poor diet (which includes excessive sugar, fats, and carbohydrates), lack of exercise or discipline, vegetable intake, fiber absorption, stress, emotional and financial problems, and lack of proper rest and sleep, just to name a few things. Sometimes it can occur because of the effects of certain medications like steroids.

In the church world, where we have preached thousands upon thousands of messages on the evils of fornication, adultery, murder, homosexuality, church and world politics, abortion, paying your tithes and offerings, giving, treating people right, gambling, drinking, and drug and pornographic addiction, we rarely confront the BIG ELEPHANT IN THE ROOM, namely GLUTTONY. Just about every event in our lives, from bridal showers to baby showers, funerals to graduations, sporting events, you name it, involves food! Our society is inundated with food! Currently, there are approximately 336 cooking shows of all kinds. It's no wonder we have issues with food! Most commercials are for foods that are not healthy for us. You can gain 10 pounds just watching them. How do we overcome this GLUTTONOUS SPIRIT that has even crept into our churches? "How so?" you may ask. In a physical manner, some churches (in an effort support the church ministry) sell chicken, fish dinners, and desserts of all kinds. In a spiritual manner, The Body of Christ (in some respects) has been guilty of preaching an unbalanced message on prosperity. It's all we seem to hear. It presents prosperity in such an extreme light that we cringe when we are faced with any kind of suffering. God's people now only come to Him when they want to demand a blessing rather than BE the VERY BLESSING He and His Word desire. We are causing God's people to develop "itching ears," so that the things they really need to hear are being shunned and not put into practice.

Case in point, afflictions, fiery trials, tribulations, tests, and storms are all considered bad words that we don't want in our Christian vernacular. We only want to hear: "It's our season," "It's our turn," "It's our time." That's not to say that in some respects that isn't true, because as God's people there is an appointed time and season for our miracles, breakthroughs, deliverances, healings, and prosperity. However, we as The Body of Christ need to focus on developing and maturing in Christian character and integrity. Who are we when we leave the church building and are headed to the parking lot? Who are we when we are in the workplace? Who are we in the grocery store line and in rush hour traffic? How do we handle ourselves when we are wrongly accused? If we are so focused on RECEIVING BLESSINGS, our perception of God is incorrect. We also have a physically obese nation where one in three people are at least 10-15 pounds overweight. Our children are even more calorically deceived. They consume more junk than ever before. They don't engage in physical activity any longer. Sports, aside from watching them on television, is a rare activity in which they will participate. The only body part that receives constant activity are their thumbs, by playing video games and texting via cell phones. Consequently, their spiritual diet is lacking as well. Their emotional profile is angry, self-entitled, impatient, selfish, rebellious toward any form of authority, and hostile. While they are more intelligent when it comes to technology, they lack the life skills and character to maintain a prosperous lifestyle. They are so used to pushing a button or clicking on a screen to get their answers. They are unfamiliar with how the card catalog system in a library operates. They can easily access Google from their phone, tablet, or laptop for immediate answers and results. They are unfamiliar and inept when it comes to using a thesaurus or dictionary. Help us, Jesus! So, now that we have identified, defined, and explained HOW WE GAINED THE WEIGHT, we need help in LOSING THE WEIGHT. How do we do that?

First, you must recognize that there is weight gain (spiritually speaking). The Scripture to reference is found in the book of Hebrews, and reads as such:

Hebrews 12:1 (KJV)	"Wherefore seeing we also are compassed about with so great a cloud of witnesses, let us **lay aside every weight, and the sin which doth so easily beset us**, and let us run with patience the race that is set before us,"

You must recognize that you are treating the Word of God or church fellowship like a crack addict. You run there to get your fix. You experience your HIGH, then you keep on moving. You go back to the distractions, sins, habits, and destructive behavior that you came in with. **YES**, the presence of the Lord is enjoyable. **YES**, the choir and praise team sing you HAPPY. **YES**, the Holy Spirit really used your pastor (or appointed preacher) to minister the Word of God to your heart.

The problem is, you didn't allow it to TRANSFORM YOU, which is a condition of both the heart and mind.

As you apply Romans 12:1-2 consistently to your life, not only VERBALLY but by obeying it on a regular basis, you will see both IMMEDIATE and GRADUAL change.

Romans 12:1-2 (KJV) says, "I beseech you therefore, brethren, by the mercies of God, that ye **present your bodies a living sacrifice, holy, acceptable to God**, which is your reasonable service. **And be not conformed to this world: but be ye transformed by the renewing of your mind,** that ye may prove what is that good, and acceptable, and perfect will of God."

There are so many valuable "spiritual weight loss nuggets" to help get you going, and keep you spiritually healthy and fit.

Let's start with the first part of Hebrews 12:1 (KJV) where it says, "lay aside every weight." It indicates an action involving self-sacrifice and denial. Alright, I already know some of your minds shuddered and cringed at that very thought.

In the Greek, **lay aside** is translated *apotithēmi, which means "to lay aside, and put off of one's self."*

Every weight is Greek and translated ogkos which means "whatever is prominent, protuberance, bulk, mass; hence a weight, burden, or encumbrance."

These are terms of immediate action with a definite result. It's going to involve ALL of you. This will include your thoughts, intentions, decisions, and motives. You must allow your mind to be purified, especially in seasons of trials and testing. When you are in affliction and you feel burdened, the tendency is for your mind to race. You get to wondering, "Why ME? When will it end? How long must I endure this? Did I do something wrong? Am I being punished?" The answer is no, however there are things concerning weight loss we need to know.

The other important thing about maintaining healthy weight loss is the things you consume. What have you spiritually consumed? Are you eating from a good, nutritional source and spiritual table? Mind you, you can't eat everyone's food. That applies both naturally and spiritually. Your diet must be consistent with your purpose.

While you need the WHOLE counsel of God's Word, every single Scripture may not apply to your affliction. People tend to use Scripture improperly to suit their own palate. For example, if they are upset with their church ministry, they may use the following Scripture as an excuse to leave (not necessarily being led by the Holy Spirit):

Genesis 12:1 (KJV): "Now the LORD had said unto Abram, Get thee out of thy country, and from thy kindred, and from thy father's house, unto a land that I will shew thee:" That's a random example, but one that probably has been used by people who have been hurt in the church. In times like these, we must truly and honestly be ROOTED and GROUNDED in God's Word in order to walk through our storms with wisdom and maturity.

CHAPTER 5

PRAISE & WORSHIP: NECESSARY WEAPONS

In the previous chapter, we discussed how important it is to lose weight and maintain the proper spiritual diet in an effort to get through your trials, temptations, and tests. Nothing fortifies that diet or enables you to maintain a spiritually-fit mindset and appetite more than praise and worship. Praise and worship is the one thing you absolutely cannot do without!

As previously discussed in chapter four, we tend to complain, cringe, cry, moan, and bellyache when we experience our go-throughs. However, complaining will short-circuit, derail, and hinder your progress.

It reminds me of a few examples that I'll cite in this chapter. One was the children of Israel who had finally, after more than 400 years of slavery and hard bondage, been set free by the power of God. But, they weren't happy to be FREE and on their way to the Promised Land. They wanted instant success; an overnight miracle, if you will. They were so used to being abused and assaulted that their behavior reflected the same. It was their job to trust God and Moses (the leader God had raised up for them), not to be concerned with their external surroundings. Isn't it interesting how this frequently occurs? We tend to look at what's going on around us to determine our response. That devil is a LIAR!

Let's examine a little more closely the events that displayed the children of Israel's responses. In Exodus 14, we encounter the children of Israel as they are en route to the Promised Land; however, this is not necessarily the route they planned on taking. They had just made their exit from Egypt and crossed the desert, only to be entrapped by the Red Sea before them and Pharaoh, along with his chariots, behind them. At this juncture, they are frightened, paranoid, frustrated, and angry all at the same time. They are now taking these emotions out on their fearless leader, Moses.

Exodus 14:11-12 (KJV): "And they said unto Moses, Because there were no graves in Egypt, hast thou taken us away to die in the wilderness? wherefore hast thou dealt thus with us, to carry us forth out of Egypt? Is not this the word that we did tell thee in Egypt, saying, Let us alone, that we may serve the Egyptians? For it had been better for

us to serve the Egyptians, than that we should die in the wilderness."

Wow! They certainly said a MOUTHFUL, huh? In our vernacular, it would be, "How you gonna leave a brother or sista hanging out to dry? You leaving us out here to DIE in the desert. Who gave you the permission slip to take us out HERE, OF ALL PLACES? We would rather be in bondage and serve the Egyptians than die here in the wilderness!" There are a couple of factors in this account I found interesting. One was how Moses addressed the situation, and how the children of Israel handled the situation. While the children of Israel responded in FEAR and FOOLISHNESS with both their thinking and their actions, Moses took the approach of FAITH. It can be extremely difficult to praise God when you're not close to Him. It doesn't mean you have all the answers but what you'll soon discover is that the Lord has a GREAT TRACK RECORD in every trying situation that concerns you. So, going back to this account, Moses stood in front of the Red Sea, surefooted, filled with faith and the rod of God in his hand. Mind you, there were 600 chosen chariots of Pharaoh with captains over each and every one of them. That can be just a bit intimidating, don't you think? Let me say without hesitation, delay, or intimidation that there's nothing wrong, sinful, or unbiblical about feeling the emotion of FEAR! Where the sinfulness comes into play is when you allow fear to rule, dominate, intimidate, or overwhelm you to the place where you don't believe the God of your salvation. This same God has continuously and faithfully removed you from dangerous situations in times past, especially when you made bad and foolish choices. Look at those times when you were a kid and hitch-hiked down dangerous, dark, and creepy roads. Look at those times when you inhaled and digested drugs or alcohol into your body, not knowing the outcome. Think about the times when you laid in strange beds (with strange people) not knowing what bodily fluids or sexually transmitted disease you could obtain. Even in your sinful choices, decisions, and direction, God COVERED YOU in His grace, mercy, and love. THIS IS WHERE YOU SHOULD INSERT A HIGH PRAISE! Oh how He loves you! Ok, back to our account. This is not something we want to hear, but the Lord will use people, even to the point of hardening their hearts, because He has a purpose. His purpose always includes dealing with your emotions and responses for His glory. Side note: Great character always comes through GREAT SUFFERING and GREAT AFFLICTION. What will you allow God to do both IN and THROUGH you during your season of suffering, trials, tests, or affliction? Will you allow it to make you BITTER or BETTER? You can ALMOST ALWAYS tell those who are "going through," because they don't hesitate to get on the phone and whine, moan, and complain about their circumstances, expecting pity. Don't get me wrong, there's nothing wrong with VENTING. By all means, get it out of your system, but DON'T STAY THERE. Learn how to "dust yourself off." When I'm in my trial, I like to think about how

Job responded. This man lost absolutely everything that was both NEAR and DEAR to him—his children, his possessions, his cattle, his livestock, etc. He was hit with simultaneous and consecutive afflictions and attacks (five to be exact). And what do you think, pray tell, was his response? Let's look.

His response was recorded in Job 1:20-21 (KJV):

"Then Job arose, and **rent his mantle,** and **shaved his head,** and **fell down upon the ground, and worshipped**, And said, Naked came I out of my mother's womb, and naked shall I return thither: the LORD gave, and the LORD hath taken away; **blessed be the name of the LORD.**" Now, this part is what truly BLESSED ME—Job 1:22 (KJV) says, "In all this Job sinned not, nor charged God foolishly."

What an awesome testimony that is! Job addressed his trials in a tripart fashion—naturally, emotionally, and spiritually. Naturally, he "rent his mantle" (tore his clothes). Whenever someone "rent their mantle," it was a sign of emotional release when someone died. Interestingly enough, because mantles were precious and valuable, the rending of the garments was the authorized expression of grief, as indicated in Leviticus 10:6. Shaving the head was another, less usual but still not uncommon, sign of grief forbidden under the Law of the Jews (Leviticus 21:5; Deuteronomy 14:1), but widely practiced by the Gentiles (Isaiah 15:2; Jeremiah 47:5; Jeremiah 48:37). Even though Job started with an understandable and natural human response, he shifted his efforts to a productive and fruitful praise and worship experience! Job also did something that we should ALL DO when we go through—he DID NOT CHARGE GOD FOOLISHLY. In other words, he didn't blame God for what he was going through. Don't allow your circumstances to consume you or let the enemy deceive you into thinking that the Lord did this to you because of sinfulness, etc. Whatever situation you are in, it is for HIS PURPOSE and He ALLOWED IT to build GODLY CHARACTER in you! Job took the time to recognize who he was and his state, then he recognized what the Lord does, and most importantly, who God is! The name of the Lord is BLESSED! Yes, right in the midst of your pain, in the midst of your storm, in the midst of your heartache, in the midst of your stress, struggle, strain, warfare, wrestling… God is THERE… and the name of the Lord is BLESSED! Knowing that His name is GREAT (powerful, mighty, and awesome), say the NAME OF JESUS. You must be as intimate as a man is with his wife. When a man is intimate with his wife and they make love, they PHYSICALLY and EMOTIONALLY become ONE FLESH. You must (make it mandatory) draw close and YET EVEN CLOSER to your heavenly Father, through His Son—Jesus. It is then, and only then, that you will experience JOY unspeakable and full of glory, and PEACE that passes all understanding. There have been many instances when I didn't know the outcome, the means of provision, or the answer, but through my consistent time in PRAYER (not just talking to the Lord and rattling off your laundry list of things for Him to do, but HEARING

His heart and His direction), I received His peace and joy. If you're waiting for people to provide you with peace and joy, you will be shortchanged and disappointed every time! Not only do we need to develop a habit of drawing close, but we need to develop a habit of TRUSTING HIM completely, for anything and absolutely EVERYTHING! In our society, trust is not something that comes very easily. It is something that must be earned and proven.

CHAPTER 6

DEALING WITH DIVORCE

One of the most difficult and painful things to ever endure is the affliction of divorce. Nothing is more heart-wrenching or has such a profound effect on your life. When you first marry, your intention is to marry for LIFE! You don't ever anticipate that divorce would even be in your vocabulary. Your mind flashed back to when you took your vows in your beautiful wedding attire in front of God, family, and friends. You then made that lifetime commitment. And when it all went south, the words became laced with a pain that's unreal.

I remember back in December 2003 when my former husband decided he no longer wanted to be married. I received the phone call at work. I literally couldn't believe what was happening. I fought back tears of shock. Yes, we had problems like all marriages. We had our arguments, etc., but this was like being PUNCHED IN THE GUT. My heart experienced one of the most crushing blows ever. I thought about how unloved and rejected I felt. Not only that, I thought about how my children and I would make it. I had two babies, ages three and one. The one-year-old was just learning how to walk. I didn't know where we were going to live, how I was going to feed my children, and how I would endure the reactions and comments of family, church members, and friends.

Because of the situation, we were forced to live in my mother's small apartment on three small sofas in her living room. We stayed with her, for just under two years, until we were financially able to afford our own place.

Even after our move, I dealt with much sadness and loneliness. It was a daily battle. I felt so much betrayal from him leaving both me and our family. It's not that he was a bad person, but I wondered how he could do this to me. I felt ugly. I felt like the kid that doesn't get picked to be on the basketball team. What was so wrong with me that he didn't want to stay with me? Why didn't he want to love me anymore? What about our children? Then, the light came ON (by way of the Holy Spirit).

One of the things the Holy Spirit spoke to me was to "LET HIM GO." (I'll cover this later in this chapter.) It was then and only then that I began to experience the peace of God. At the beginning of my separation and impending divorce, I had no desire to reconcile or even entertain the option of remarrying. That's just how hurt and angry I was. There may be someone reading this who is going through something very similar. There is great encouragement and hope for you during this very difficult and painful season. You are about to walk into another beautiful exchange. You are going to exchange your former spouse (estranged or ex-spouse) for a new and better husband. This husband will love you beyond your wildest dreams, and provide comfort and security that you've never known. Let's go to the Word.

Isaiah 54:4-8 (KJV) records, "Fear not; for thou shalt not be ashamed: neither be thou confounded; for thou shalt not be put to shame: for thou shalt forget the shame of thy youth, and shalt not remember the reproach of thy widowhood any more. For thy Maker is thine husband; the Lord of hosts is his name; and thy Redeemer the Holy One of Israel; The God of the whole earth shall he be called. For the Lord hath called thee as a woman forsaken and grieved in spirit, and a wife of youth, when thou wast refused, saith thy God. For a small moment have I forsaken thee; but with great mercies will I gather thee. In a little wrath I hid my face from thee for a moment; but with everlasting kindness will I have mercy on thee, saith the Lord thy Redeemer."

If nothing else completely describes a person who's going through a separation or divorce this DOES. Wow! Let's do a breakdown verse by verse, starting at verse four. The first part gives a command… DO NOT FEAR. I know that sounds like a crazy request when that's the first response you feel after recognizing that you're going through a divorce or separation. Fear in this verse, according to www.dictionary.com, means "to be fearful, be dreadful, or to be terrified." Fear tends to make us RUN from the pain of a situation. It seems easier at times just to GET AWAY from it. I think that's what happens when people are faced with suicidal tendencies. They just want an escape from their present reality. Before I continue with the breakdown of these Scriptures, I wanted to do a sidebar. If you know of someone who has shown signs of suicidal tendencies, make haste to help them. Time is of the essence. I've never seen so much depression, suicide, and emotional brokenness before this generation. You can have them call 1-800-273-TALK (8255) for help.

As a friend, please don't make the mistake a lot of Christians make and overly spiritualize their circumstances. What they're feeling is REAL to them. We don't need to minimize their pain or their present reality. There are too many pastors, teachers, evangelists, prophets, ministers, counsellors, or whatever we title ourselves, who lack discernment, love, compassion, and wisdom when it comes to dealing with people's pain. We tend to approach people out of insensitivity, judgment, criticism, and based on our personal experiences. We need to be very prayerful. We need to listen to the Holy Spirit for instruction. We tend to come across like Job's "friends" after their initial week of silence. We have all kinds of assumptions regarding why people are feeling a certain way, or going through their various circumstances. Yet, if it were us, we would want compassion and mercy in our tests and troubles.

Ok, let's get back to verse four before I ramble on with my own do's and don'ts list for handling people in trouble and affliction. Verse four reads, "Fear not; for thou shalt not be ashamed: neither be thou confounded; for thou shalt not be put to shame: for thou shalt forget the shame of thy youth, and shalt not remember the reproach of thy widowhood any more" (KJV). It's very interesting that the first emotion we seem to experience when we are going through something is FEAR. So, God in His love and wisdom for us, instructs us FIRST and FOREMOST… NOT TO FEAR. Whenever we are faced with adversity, hardships, tests, or obstacles, fear is our knee-jerk reaction. It's almost second nature for our human side. However, the Lord would not give us an INSTRUCTION without giving us EMPOWERMENT. It was DO NOT FEAR. Let's look at what FEAR is. In this verse, according to Strong's Concordance, it's the Hebrew word *yare'*, which is defined as "to be fearful, be dreadful, to cause astonishment and awe, be held in awe." It also means "to make afraid, terrify."

A divorce is a very frightening and traumatic experience. Oftentimes, you feel abandoned, rejected, and alone. Your mind starts racing and thinking of all kinds of things. Those things can be anything from how you're going to take care of your children and other financial obligations, to wondering if anyone will love you again. There is a love that the Lord has for you that will exceed the love of a spouse. You don't need to be terrified or feel dread because, as the Lord promised in Isaiah 54:4, you will not be ashamed. The Hebrew word for ashamed is ***buwsh***, which means "to feel shame, to be ashamed, disconcerted, disappointed." There is no disappointment in Christ. He never fails or disappoints us. It doesn't matter what we face. This verse goes on to say, "neither be thou confounded." The Hebrew word for confounded is ***kalam***. This exhortation was for the person not to be humiliated, insulted, or ashamed. People that experience divorce oftentimes feel as if they are second or third class citizens. Some may even feel as if they are damaged goods. Divorce even shatters further the hearts of those who have been married multiple times. Their heart requires an even more delicate touch and handling from the Lord.

I recall being bewildered, alone, frustrated, and scared. However, the Lord was so faithful to me. I remember Him sweetly speaking to me (even though I didn't understand it at the time), "LET HIM GO." Most women tend to be eternal optimists, and try to fix abusive and destructive relationships. My marriage was indeed just that! Even though I loved my husband a great deal, there was a lot of verbal and mental turmoil that I endured on a regular basis. I thought we would be able to work through anything. I believed with all my heart he was "The One," "My Soulmate." But, that didn't matter once he "lowered the boom." Going through my divorce was a very tumultuous time and a transitional season. Everything from physical residence, financial questions, insecurities, and marital status came into play. I praise God that regardless of what took place during that season, He was with me not only to provide for me, but to love me beyond my wildest dreams. It was a season of trust. When the Lord said in His Word that I wouldn't be ASHAMED… He was absolutely right! I am His beloved daughter who is valued and beautiful in His sight. I am the apple of His eye. The same applies to the one who is reading this. No matter how painful this adjustment is, it will progressively get better as you yield your broken heart and spirit to the Lord for Him to heal and mend. Sometimes it doesn't feel that way, especially when you have children who have gotten used to being around that spouse. It's particularly difficult when you need support and they are not there. Then, there are the lonely nights and the now COLD SIDE of the bed that is more prominent. Where is the spouse that vowed to love, comfort, keep, and be faithful to you "for richer, for poorer, in sickness and in health"? It's rough to deal with, and even though we are Christians we still endure very HUMAN experiences and ordeals. Divorce or separation is one of them. The great thing to know is that ALL IS NOT LOST. I want to encourage those who are in this season to draw close to the Lord. I also want to encourage you to connect with a loving and supportive prayer group. Mind you, every prayer group is NOT for you. Some people are busybodies who just want to feed their own insecure flesh with the details of what happened in your marriage. Seek the Lord and ask Him to show you who you can confide in and trust. Also, ask Him to show you where you can go for provision (if needed). You are NOT ALONE. There is help out there. Don't be ashamed to ask for it. It can come from your church ministry, a family member, or a close friend. I believe firmly when the Word says, "you have not, because you ask not" (James 4:2, KJV 2000). A lot of people don't mind helping, but they aren't given an opportunity because people are too ashamed or embarrassed to simply ask. Remember the worst thing a person can ever tell you is NO. With every NO, there is a YES somewhere.

Also, make sure you get OUT. Go to a park, take up an exercise class, get a pedicure, or do something that makes you feel beautiful. You deserve that! Be very cautious about the advice you hear, and be selective about what you receive. Everything isn't for you. You'll discover many people will try and convey their well-meaning advice from their situations to fit your situation. That may NOT work. Simply thank others for their concern, encourage them to pray for you, and KEEP IT MOVING. That's not being mean or rude; you really need to be selective and discerning, especially when your emotions are raw and vulnerable. It doesn't mean you don't love folks or appreciate them, but your ear needs to be sensitive to the Spirit of the Lord for clarity, healing, and direction.

This is a new, but difficult season. You will make it! You will get through it. Many have gone through similar situations and died. But, you are STILL HERE, and God has a purpose for you in the midst of it all.

CHAPTER 7

DEALING WITH REJECTION, LONELINESS, AND BEING MISUNDERSTOOD

One of the most difficult things to endure when going through affliction is dealing with rejection. We all, at some point, have dealt with being rejected. It could have started in your childhood, particularly if you were abandoned or not properly loved. It may have manifested itself in the form of not making the cheerleading squad, debate or football team. It also may have shown up in the form of not being asked to go to the senior prom by the person to whom you were attracted.

Rejection is something NO ONE likes. Even those who show a certain level of maturity and try to laugh it off don't like it. Rejection (according to the Merriam-Webster Dictionary) is defined as "refusal, spurning, dismissal, elimination."

In our society and on our TV shows, rejection is commonplace. During any given week, we see a person on *The Real Housewives of Atlanta*, *American Idol*, or *The Voice* being eliminated for lack of execution, unpopularity, or just because. Our culture has become acclimated to people getting the ax. It's no wonder that an all-time high of 16 percent of high schoolers have considered suicide. Let's take a quick look at the suicide facts reported on www.nobullying.com:

Almost 5,000 lives are lost each year due to suicide. Almost half of the suicides that occur are done using firearms, with suffocation coming in at a close second, and poison falling in at third. About 13 percent of those created a plan while about eight percent actually followed through within a year. Boys have a higher possibility of committing suicide. Of the reported suicides in the youth age-range, around 80 percent were male, while only 20 percent were female. At the same time, however, girls are much more likely to report an attempted or thought of suicide than boys are. Native Americans and Alaskans have the highest rate of suicide among the races. The survey showed that Hispanics are more likely to report thoughts of suicide or an attempt than non-Hispanics. It is thought that around 25 suicide attempts are made for every successful suicide.

Those statistics indicate to me that there are a lot of people in pain. There are some obviously willing to say they need help, while others suffer in silence. We need the Holy Spirit to give us discernment regarding those who are going through in our homes, jobs, schools, and other places so that we can effectively minister to them.

Who do you know that feels unloved? Who do you know that might need a listening ear? There are some people who might be battling the spirit of rejection or depression. It can be something as simple as a hug or smile that is needed. Roots of rejection tend to run deep.

I was the firstborn, so initially I received a lot of attention. Of course, as I gained two very beautiful sisters, the attention was diverted to them. If you are like me and you're not careful or secure, you will tend to feel neglected. Your time is now being shared between parents, grandparents, aunts, uncles, brothers, and cousins.

If anyone can identify with REJECTION, it is Jesus HIMSELF. He is well aware of the feelings of being betrayed, neglected, and abandoned. Let's go to the Word to be more specific.

Isaiah 53:5 (KJV) says, "He is despised and rejected of men; a man of sorrows, and acquainted with grief: and we hid as it were our faces from him; he was despised, and we esteemed him not."

Let me break down each aspect of the way Jesus was treated by both God and man. I'm going to start with man. In the first part of Isaiah 53:5 it says He was "DESPISED." That is the Hebrew word **bazah**, which means "to regard with contempt, to be despicable, to be vile or worthless." Next, He was "REJECTED OF MEN." This is the Hebrew phrase **chadel 'iysh**, which means "rejected, forbearing, transient, fleeting, lacking, made destitute or forsaken by mankind, human, whosoever." Going further, the Bible indicates that Jesus was a man of sorrows. "What's that?" you might ask, or some might know. But for those of us who are a little less educated, let me school you. Jesus is a man who endured and experienced both physical and mental pain. Sorrows in the Hebrew is translated **makob**. Speaking as someone who hates needles and IV's, I can't in my wildest imagination fathom the beating and crucifixion He suffered JUST FOR ME. Oh what an awesome and great love the Lord has for ME!

The sorrows Jesus endured go way beyond the piddly little complaints we generally have. We tend to make huge mountains out of molehills. We complain about our aches, pains, job issues, relationship troubles, etc. Not to minimize what we are enduring, but it pales in comparison to the physical, emotional, and mental suffering our Lord and Savior encountered. The thought of Him being beaten beyond recognition, the crown of thorns jammed into His precious skull, and the agonizing crucifixion of His hands and feet totally baffles my imagination. He took His beaten, bloodied, mangled, and torn body 650 yards (equivalent to a little more than the length of five football fields), while carrying a 110 pound cross and being verbally assaulted by the very ones who exclaimed "Hosanna" just one week prior.

The suffering you may be enduring may be great and almost seem to be too much to handle, but trust me, the Lord has allowed it for His purpose. Sometimes our suffering can be because of our poor decisions, impatience, or presumption. Other times, God has divinely ordered it. I want to remind you about our brother Job. In Job 1, Job was minding his own business and enjoying his family when trouble came. Mind you, Job was one who feared God and eschewed evil. Fearing God meant that Job reverenced and respected the presence of the Lord. He eschewed evil, meaning, he avoided and turned aside from sin. He put it away from him. In other words, he was a man that truly loved God. He didn't play when it came to his relationship with God. It seems very strange and doesn't make sense that he would have to lose his children, his property, his sheep and cattle, and then on top of that have to deal with a debilitating disease. It just didn't seem fair. You might even feel as though the hand you've been dealt doesn't seem fair. This may sound extremely insensitive, but it doesn't have to be fair in order to serve God's purpose.

You are on assignment. There are things God is working out in you during this season. You are probably wondering, "What in God's name could that be?" Well, James 1:2 (KJV) says that we are to "count it all joy." That's probably the last thing we want to do when we're going through problems, tests, temptations, and trials. You might be saying to yourself, "How could I possibly feel joyful during a time like this? My body aches. I got an evil report from the doctor. My children and family are falling apart. My supervisor is giving me the blues. My finances are in shambles, and I have more MONTH than I do MONEY. What in the world is going on?" Well, "counting it all joy" doesn't mean you act as if nothing is happening and you walk around on the clouds aimlessly like some angel. No, it simply means you change your mindset (we will address this further in the next chapter). It means your response is to look to the Lord as opposed to you handling the situation by your own means or methods. In Greek, the word count is translated ***hegeomai***. It means the following: 1) to lead; 2) to go before; 3) to be a leader; 4) to rule, command; 5) to have authority over (like a prince of regal power, governor, viceroy, chief, leading as respects influence, controlling in counsel, overseers or leaders of the churches; 6) any kind of leader, chief, commander; 7) the leader in speech, chief speaker, spokesman; and 8) to consider, deem, account, think. That's a mouthful, right there! In essence, we determine how we are going to respond to our circumstances, not the Lord. Our mindset typically (and expectedly) is to get angry, upset, and depressed. However, we have a God who not only cares about our circumstances, but cares for and loves us in the midst of our circumstances.

There's not a situation that is a surprise to Him. You didn't shock Him when you lost your spouse, your job, your child, etc. He knew about it before the foundations of the world. Consequently, if He knew about your situation, He obviously knows the outcome. The outcome for you is going to be fantastic! There are some things, however, that He must build up in your character before that fantastic outcome. Let's go back to the book of James to find out what He wants to do in you.

It says in James 1:3 (KJV) "that the **trying** of your faith worketh patience." That means, according to the Greek definition of trying, ***dokimion***, "the PROVING of your faith." It also means "that by which something is tried or proved, a test." Let's give a natural example. You know when you're cooking or baking something, you add all the required ingredients for a certain recipe? Well, the person that's there assisting you (usually called the sous chef) may taste the meal or dessert and will tell you if it needs something else. Sometimes if you put too much of one ingredient and not enough of another, it can fall flat, like when you're baking a cake. I know, for example, I'm not the best pancake maker (at least from scratch) at all! I often go the shortcut route and use the kind that says, "JUST ADD WATER." Don't judge me. Even with that process, I must follow the directions by the letter in order for it to turn out right. Any deviation could result in mushy, batter-filled, nasty pancakes. That's NO GOOD for any of the hungry and greedy folks in my house! So, **trying** entails understanding the value of the process. Process (not my favorite word) is something we live by every day. It takes process to get up in the morning, get dressed, groom yourself, get in your car, drive in traffic to your place of employment or school, get out of the vehicle, walk into work, logon to your computer via username and password, and then proceed to your normal activities, only to log out and do the reverse all over again for a normal five day (ten day bi-weekly) pay period. I'm inclined to believe **PROCESS** stands for the following:

Procedures
Regimented
Occurring
Consistently
Executing
Systematic
Standards

It takes TIME to do anything successfully. I'm so used to wanting to take shortcuts, but nine times out of ten, the Lord will put me in reverse and tell me, "Back it up, Daughter, there's something I want you to learn." Also, there are valuable things you learn by doing things step-by-step in the Spirit.

You never truly GET IT if things are either just handed to you or given to you in the form of a shortcut. I'm guilty, and so is my son. We are always trying to go from A to Z in 60 seconds, when the Lord often takes His sweet time in preparing me to learn something. While my flesh is struggling, at the end of learning whatever lesson, I'm thankful He took the time to instruct me.

The one thing a GREAT PARENT does is instruct their children. Let's go to the Word for confirmation of this.

Exodus 18:20 (God's instruction to Moses for the children of Israel) says, "And thou shalt teach them ordinances and laws, and shalt shew them the way wherein they must walk, and the work that they must do" (KJV).

The one thing human beings are equipped from birth to do is LEARN. We learn everything from how to feed ourselves, to walking, talking, running, riding a bike, combing our hair, and bathing ourselves, just to name a few. Unfortunately, because we are in such a rushed and technologically-based society, we want instantaneous EVERYTHING. We've lost the love of LEARNING. We've lost the art of process and procedure. Consequently, the Lord must slow us down to teach us. Can I get a witness?

My mind goes to young children and how excited they become when they take their first steps. In the beginning, they are crawling, creeping, and learning how to stand. As they learn to stand on their own, we as their parents might hold one or both of their hands until we begin to see that they are strong enough to walk on their own. They will extend one leg, then the other, and as they put one foot in front of the other, they develop stronger faith and confidence in their ability to walk. As we let go, they will totter, and may initially sit down. But, as we face them and tell them, "Walk to me. You CAN DO IT!" they start to walk further and further until they walk into your arms. They walk right into the arms of the one that loves them. The same occurs when you're going through whatever process or procedure the Lord is using to educate you.

He may tell you, "You can do ALL THINGS through Christ who strengthens you." He will echo and whisper His Word in your heart and spirit, which will build your faith and trust in Him. One thing you need to remember as you grow and go through stages and processes is that you are His prized possession. You are the very one He suffered, died, and rose victoriously for. You are always on His mind. You are the reason He left glory, grew in the womb of a 13-year-old virgin (conceived by the Holy Spirit), walked the earth as a man, and endured suffering that no other man has experienced throughout the annals of time. You are the expression of His never-ending, never-failing, faithful love. You are the treasure of His heart. He loves you past your wildest dreams and most vivid imagination. Don't despise the things you are learning. I have said it before, and I'll freely say it again, I've always been the one who's famous for trying to locate a shortcut or easy way out, when in fact, the Savior is teaching me the valuable lesson of PROCESS.

Process is never easy, desired, or expected. In our society, we want it quick, and we want it NOW. In the mind of God, it's simply not going to happen that way. In yielding to the PROCESS (governed by the Holy Spirit), you learn and master life-changing habits, strategies, management skills, leadership ability, and humility. You learn like never before to walk in the fruit of the Spirit. Your character and heart are being sharpened and developed so they can be utilized for the kingdom of God.

You no longer belong to yourself. You belong to the Lord, and it's His purposes you are obligated to fulfill.

There may be one thing or 100 things the Lord will try to teach you in the process of your life. It could be something as simple as balancing a checkbook, creating and maintaining a budget for your household, eating and preparing healthy foods for your family, exercising consistently to lose and maintain a healthy weight, and so on. We are also in an era of Christendom where prosperity is preached incorrectly. There are those who preach "name it and claim it" and "blab it and grab it" as if we are supposed to get whatever we want just because we say it. We treat God like a cosmic Santa Claus or a Genie we rub out of a lamp to get what we want. That's not how the PROCESS works. He's God! He's the POTTER, we are the CLAY. We need to submit to His molding, shaping, and fashioning.

One of the most exasperating things I've encountered as a parent of two teenagers is that they feel because they've grown to a certain height and are developing physically in certain areas, they can dictate to me what they want, when they want it, and how they want it. Not so! As a parent, it's my desire to BLESS my children and provide them with GREAT THINGS! It cracks me up how my son asks for the most recent video games for his Xbox, when his chores haven't been completed or his grades aren't up to par. Then, he huffs and gets angry when I don't comply with his demands. My daughter is the same way when she wants what she wants. I can only LAUGH! They don't determine how and when their desires are fulfilled. The same goes for us in our relationship with God. If there are things He has ordained and promised us, He will deliver them to us in His good timing, after we have fulfilled the faithful and consistent obedience He requires. If we give our children what they want when they don't necessarily deserve it, we'd be guilty of ENABLING them instead of educating them on the blessing of being THANKFUL and living OBEDIENT lives.

CHAPTER 8

DEALING WITH THE BATTLE BETWEEN MY EARS (MY MIND)

One of the biggest challenges of the day is the thousands upon thousands of thoughts that run through our minds—What are we going to wear to work? How are we going to pay our bills? What are we preparing for dinner? And so on. So, it stands to reason, those thoughts accelerate when you're battling and going through tests and trials.

The average brain weighs about 3.03 pounds or 48.5 ounces. There are 43 blood vessels that operate and function in the brain. The main blood vessel that flows to the brain is called the carotid artery. Its function is to make sure that blood flows properly and adequate oxygen and circulation are maintained.

The brain is without a doubt a necessary organ for the human body. Without it, no other bodily operations can take place. If you are decapitated, everything else in the body ceases to function.

Let's take a spiritual spin on this as well. You are what you THINK you are. What you allow to PROCESS in your mind, determines your outcome. Let's go to the Word of God to further discuss.

Proverbs 23:7 (KJV) says, "For as he thinketh in his heart, so is he:" The Hebrew word for thinketh is ***sha'ar*** (pronounced shah-air), and it means "to split open, to calculate, to estimate, to reason, to reckon." Your mind is a busy machine. You must use that mind that God blessed you with to think the way Jesus thought, which brought glory to God. With that same mind, you can also accomplish God's will and purpose for your life.

For so many years our minds have been tainted and poisoned with word curses (we discussed that a couple of chapters back), so sometimes it's difficult to move forward until we see that our thinking is what's held us back so long. Joyce Meyer calls it "stinking thinking." If you can change your MIND, you can change your LIFE.

What negative thoughts have bombarded your mind lately? Thoughts of failure, insecurity, suicide, depression, financial woes, family and relational issues, job or supervisor problems, health challenges? You can change the way you respond to these by CHANGING YOUR MIND. "How do I do that?" you may wonder. Well, let us take our trek back to the Word of God. It's in the Word of God that we find all we need pertaining to how we live, obtain, and maintain success.

Every thought doesn't need to be entertained. As I previously stated, we receive thousands of thoughts and impulses every day. According to the Huffington Post, we receive an average of 50,000-70,000 thoughts per day! That's 3,000 per hour, 50 per minute, and just under one per second. Whoa, no wonder we struggle in our minds so much! Thankfully, we have a God who created our mind and understands quite well how it operates.

2 Corinthians 10:3-5 (KJV) says, "For though we walk in the flesh, we do not war after the flesh: (For the weapons of our warfare are not carnal, but mighty through God to the pulling down of strong holds;) Casting down imaginations, and every high thing that exalteth itself against the knowledge of God, and bringing into captivity every thought to the obedience of Christ."

In our English language, that would read (my paraphrase): "Even though we have a fleshly mind and body, we don't operate with fleshly methods because the weapons God gives us aren't fleshly, but are given through Him to pull down strongholds. We can now throw down imaginations that have held us back for so long. We've had to contend with thoughts of suicide, lust, murder, hatred, anger, rage, wrath, frustration, and depression, just to name a few; however, we don't have to live like that any longer."

This will not be easy, but it can be done! It will take consistent practice and verbal assaults (utilizing the Word of God in every circumstance) to obtain successful, complete, and thorough victory. Think of the circumstance(s) that drove you to read this book. How did you handle it? Did you break something? Did you throw something across the room? Did you cuss somebody out? Did you slash tires? Did you key somebody's car? What did you do? Was it the result you wanted? Was it the result God desired for your life? Sometimes we can do the WRONG THING for the RIGHT REASON, so it will yield NOTHING FRUITFUL. As I stated before, it will take great and persistent practice, but your verbal response must come from the very heart of God to yield the results you desire.

Jesus was no stranger to trouble. Matthew 4:1-10 gives the account of when Jesus was led of the Holy Spirit into the wilderness to be tempted of the devil. Doesn't seem to make much sense that you would be "led of the Holy Spirit... to be tempted of the devil." It almost sounds like an oxymoron, huh? But, as with everything else we face in our lives, there is a purpose to this seemingly strange event.

Let's look at what a wilderness is overall. It's not what you would call a nice place for a vacation. It's not somewhere you would go to relax or take your family. It's not a place that's very productive or fruitful, or is it? Wilderness is mentioned in the

Scriptures 305 times within 294 verses. Typically, a wilderness is a desert place. It is a lonely region or a place that is considered an uncultivated region fit for pasturage. However, it seems as though whenever God wants to speak in a powerful way, teach a lesson, or reveal himself, He always seems to do it in a WILDERNESS or a SOLITARY PLACE. He can't afford to contend with the distractions you encounter on a day-to-day basis. Social media (Facebook, Instagram, Snapchat, Periscope, Twitter), TV, your job, church ministry, family, spouse, etc., can be major hindrances to you effectively hearing the voice of the Lord. So often, just like Jesus, you are DRIVEN into the desert (wilderness). It is a place where your senses are put to the test and your flesh is in REAL, LIVE, predatory danger. The wilderness is a place of absolute vulnerability. Many parts of you are exposed to the elements, loneliness, fears, and other threats.

In the Judean wilderness, there are at least 10-20 types of animals that can cause harm to a person who is exposed to the environment of the wilderness. The amazing thing is that Jesus, who was 100 percent human yet 100 percent God, was in the environment of these wild animals. Everything from hyenas, to ibexes (a form of wild goat), to toads and frogs, snakes, insects, wild birds, bears, cheetahs, and lions were within proximity and had unexpected access to Jesus at any time. The same is true when we deal with life's trials, tests, and afflictions. Most times, they are unexpected and all of the time they are unwanted. Yet, the Lord uses them to bring out the best in us. They are there to keep us humble. They are used to cause us to appreciate the goodness of God, His infinite grace and mercy, and oftentimes, His abundant provision. With that said, the following lessons are to be learned while in your place of wilderness and solitude. 1) You were separated with a purpose and that was to hear God in an undistracted way. God is faithful in allowing your friends, your haters, that unruly boss, those irritating people, those unsatisfied church members, and the spouse and children who always need something to PUSH and DRIVE you into the presence of the only one who can do something and anything about your circumstances. 2) The wilderness shows what you are truly made of. It shows who you truly are! Your identity will be tested to its breaking point. The enemy will come at you while you are in the wilderness and call you everything but what God called you. He will challenge your identity every chance he gets. He doesn't care about what God said you are, what you will be, or anything of the sort. He wants you insecure, fearful, and unbelieving. He's counting on you to count yourself out. In the wilderness, those fears can be intensified. 3) Jesus was sharpening His skills in spiritual warfare by vocally employing the Word of God every single time the enemy came against Him. Know that when you are in your wilderness, the enemy is not only after your IDENTITY, but your AUTHORITY (IN CHRIST), and your WORSHIP. If he can get you to lose sight of any of these, you're already defeated. Jesus not only recognized who He was, but He also understood the power in which He operated, the authority He was given, and the person He worshipped! As a result of that, and His willingness to submit to the Spirit of God, the devil left Him, and the angels of the Lord came and ministered to Him. (See Matthew 4:11). While in your wilderness season, it's also important for you to note that there is always PROVISION and a way is always made, especially when that is where the Lord has directed your steps. Isaiah 43:19 (KJV) says, "Behold, I will do a new thing; now it shall spring forth; shall ye not know it? I will even make a way in the wilderness, and rivers in the desert." You will come out victorious upon your exit from the wilderness. You will be more powerful, stronger, and wiser. It is only then that you will excel in your ministry, your relationships, your career, and everything else concerning you. You are also putting the devil on notice that your God is MORE POWERFUL than he is, and that He will always come through for you.

As I discussed in a previous chapter, don't try to avoid the process; the wilderness is the next step to your spiritual elevation. You can't go around it, avoid it, or curtail it. If Jesus, the Son of the living God, had to go through the wilderness, what makes you think you DON'T? We often want to be anointed, gifted, etc., but seldom want the purging, refining, training, and schooling that precedes the elevation. It simply must happen that way. Your ability to keep your mind stayed on Christ and meditate on the Word of God is paramount in this season. It will assure your victory. You will appreciate the love God has for you after your season in the wilderness. He hasn't left or abandoned you. He was there all the time!

CHAPTER 9

OVERCOMING BARRENNESS

One of the most difficult seasons you will ever have to encounter and deal with in your walk with God is the season of BARRENNESS. "What is BARRENNESS?" you may ask. Well, according to www.dictionary.com it means: 1) not producing or incapable of producing offspring; sterile; 2) unproductive; unfruitful; 3) without capacity to interest or attract; 4) mentally unproductive, dull, stupid; 5) not producing results; fruitless; 6) destitute, bereft, lacking.

That's some pretty rough terminology. As a matter of fact, no one on the planet would be happy about this description. Why is that? Well, it has always been in the mind and heart of God for anything He created to "Be FRUITFUL, and MULTIPLY" (Genesis 1:22, KJV). He never made anything to last just for a little while. If you notice, we were all created with the capacity and ability to REPRODUCE, REPLICATE, and DUPLICATE (after our own kind, of course). Even though you are unique, you are designed with a purpose to do and become MORE. Sometimes, whether through medical challenges or life's circumstances, it seems like even your greatest efforts don't yield the harvest you intended. As a matter of fact, in the Bible, if a couple didn't have a child or multiple children, they were looked at with great disdain. The first biblical case of infertility was with Abraham and Sarah. Interestingly enough, it wasn't because Sarah was old. Sarah had a problem conceiving when she was a YOUNG woman. So, consequently, can you imagine year after year, season after season, time after time not being able to conceive and bear children? Then, you must watch and observe other women (within your community) carry and deliver children. Your emotions are all over the place. You feel neglected, forgotten, abandoned, and as if something is wrong with you. You can't endure the pain of watching another woman have a baby and nurse her child! You are not a happy camper by any stretch of the imagination. How do you handle and process all this? Well, let's look at Sarah's initial response. "And Sarai said unto Abram, Behold now, the LORD hath restrained me from bearing: I pray thee, go in unto my maid; it may be that I may obtain children by her. And Abram hearkened to the voice of Sarai. And Sarai Abram's wife took Hagar her maid the Egyptian, after Abram had dwelt ten years in the land of Canaan, and gave her to her husband Abram to be his wife. And he went in unto Hagar, and she conceived: and when she saw that she had conceived, her mistress was despised in her eyes. And Sarai said unto Abram, My wrong *be* upon thee: I have given my maid into thy bosom; and when she saw that she had conceived, I was despised in her eyes: the LORD judge between me and thee. But Abram said unto Sarai, Behold, thy maid *is* in thy hand; do to her as it pleaseth thee. And when Sarai dealt hardly with her, she fled from her face" (Genesis 16:2-6, KJV).

Here's the recap. Both Abram and Sarai (later named Abraham and Sarah) were incapable of having a baby. As a result of frustration and impatience, Sarai decided to "help God out" by inviting Hagar into her husband's bed! Talk about a dumb move. The thing you don't want to do is make a decision in your season of frustration and desperation. Long-term decisions don't need to be made in temporary circumstances. God had promised them a SON, it was up to them to WAIT and to TRUST GOD. Sarai even took it a step further by allowing Hagar to become a WIFE to Abraham. (Genesis 16:3). She allowed him to be in covenant with a person of Egypt. Hagar wasn't a part of the Promise. God, however, allowed it and here comes Ishmael. Consequently, it became a serious "Baby Mama Drama" situation that got very ugly. Abram (later called Abraham) was 86 when Ishmael was born. Sarai was 76. When Abraham was 99, the Lord spoke to him and repeated His promise as noted in Genesis 17:1-7 (KJV): "And when Abram was ninety years old and nine, the LORD appeared to Abram, and said unto him, I *am* the Almighty God; walk before me, and be thou perfect. And I will make my covenant between me and thee, and will multiply thee exceedingly. And Abram fell on his face: and God talked with him, saying, As for me, behold, my covenant *is* with thee, and thou shalt be a father of many nations. Neither shall thy name any more be called Abram, but thy name shall be Abraham; for a father of many nations have I made thee. And I will make thee exceeding fruitful, and I will make nations of thee, and kings shall come out of thee. And I will establish my covenant between me and thee and thy seed after thee in their generations for an everlasting covenant, to be a God unto thee, and to thy seed after thee."

The key to overcoming barrenness lies in your ability to remember and recall what God has promised you. If you can do that, you stand steps ahead of those who are fearful and live in doubt and unbelief. Once Sarah and Abraham got past their fleshly proclivities, they were able to produce the promised son God intended. Genesis 21:1-2 (NLT) says, "The LORD kept his word and did for Sarah exactly what he had promised. She became pregnant, and she gave birth to a son for Abraham in his old age. This happened at just the time God had said it would." The promise will manifest when you move in undeniable, faith-filled obedience.

CHAPTER 10

LETTING IT GO! OVERCOMING UNFORGIVENESS

One of the most debilitating, mind-altering things that can ever take place is when we are dealing with unforgiveness. We need to let go of everything—from that cheating spouse, to the one who spoke evil against us, to the nasty relative who inappropriately touched us! Boy, how RAW, TENDER, and RAGGED our emotions become when we've encountered some serious tragedy or circumstance. We all know people can do some horrible things to our emotions, whether intentional or not. Marriages, churches, workplace situations, college campuses have all been the dumping ground of people who have experienced both sowing and reaping the poisonous seeds of unforgiveness.

There will always be a person on this planet who will need to, at some point in their life, forgive someone. Since the beginning of time, and due to the sinfulness of mankind, forgiveness will always be needed. It was first needed in the Garden of Eden when both Adam and Eve sinned against God. It trickled down to Cain when he murdered his brother Abel, and it continued as people repeatedly did things that were contrary to the Word and will of God. Before we engage in pointing a shaming, judgmental, and self-righteous finger at those who seemingly have sinned against us, we need to exercise self-examination concerning our own sins. In an effort not to minimize the pain of our personal tragedies and experiences, we must also recognize that we too have sinned, both against God and others. We have also caused and inflicted pain, hurt, and tragedy upon those we've loved, but also to those who have mistreated us. The question remains, what will we do to break this seemingly never-ending cycle? Well, like anything in the life of a believer, it's going to be a PROCESS. Process is that seven letter word that involves tears, pain, and much prayer. Throughout this book (in particular chapter seven), I have discussed PROCESS at great length. I've always admired those who have endured great distress at the hands of others, and forgiven them with seemingly great ease. In actuality, it wasn't EASY at all. It took the grace of God to get them through. When I think of people such as John Walsh who lost his son, and Jennifer Hudson who lost her mom, nephew, and sister at the hands of heinous criminals, yet forgave, I applaud their resolve. It was in their decision to forgive that they received healing. Now, the same can and will be said for you. Who do you need to forgive? Who hurt you? Who broke your heart? Who robbed you of your peace? Who stole from you? Who rejected you? Who caused you to experience unrest in your soul and spirit? No matter who it was, you need to forgive them. You must release them from the pain they caused you. Depending on the severity of the offense, and your willingness to forgive, it's going to take some time and submission to the Spirit of God.

I like to use biblical examples and the response of Jesus. He is the first person that comes to mind because He was well-acquainted with grief and experienced betrayal and rejection at the hand of those He loved and died for.

The second person that comes to mind is Joseph. Here was a young man who was highly favored by both his father and God. Unfortunately, because of the favoritism demonstrated by his dad, Joseph encountered "haterism" or "hateration" from his older siblings. They hated him so much that they threw him into a pit, sold him into slavery, and faked his death. They didn't realize that was possibly the best thing to ever happen to Joseph. His first stop was Potiphar's house, where he was appointed to serve. Due to false allegations by Potiphar's lust-driven wife, Joseph was imprisoned for rape, sexual assault, and sexual harassment. (Those are my words, not the actual Hebrew legal terminology.) He served a sentence of roughly two years. In total, from the time he was captured as a slave until his promotion in Pharaoh's court, he served 13 years. That was a lot of time to mull over what his brothers had done to him, what Potiphar's ratchet, no-good wife had done to him, and the butler who had unintentionally forgotten him. We all have experienced some pretty rough things. Some things probably would have caused us to take our own lives. We have battled loneliness, abandonment, depression, miscarriages, divorces, abortions, job losses, financial issues, health issues, etc. Those are just a few things. Some things you haven't been able to tell anyone because they were just so overwhelming. However, you are now reading this book and you need to release the pain, trouble, and hurt to God. You survived the rape, the molestation. You made it through the poverty, the bad supervisor, the domestically violent spouse. You are a living testimony. People have killed themselves over a lot less! People need what you have, and you are in a position to be free. Joseph tested his brothers to see where their hearts were. Joseph learned (through false accusations and imprisonment) how to forgive those who wronged him. He learned the value of staying faithful and serving God. He demonstrated he could be trusted. Sometimes when we're going through, the last thing we want to do is help or minister to others. Not Joseph. He was a servant and was extremely helpful. He didn't allow his pain and traumatic series of events to overtake him with emotions. He allowed his pain to push him further into the presence of God. He had plenty of time to sit in a dank, dusty, smelly, and rat-infested prison cell and commemorate all the horrible things that befell him. However, instead of dwelling on feelings of loneliness, betrayal, rejection, unforgiveness, and self-pity, Joseph used the opportunity to be a blessing to the butler and the baker. During those dark days, God was getting him ready to minister to his family. Once the famine came to Egypt, Pharaoh had his dream, but Joseph's administrative prowess and the anointing of love and forgiveness was demonstrated to the very brothers that threw him into a pit and allowed him to be sold into slavery. You very well (at this reading) may be experiencing the hurt of those you love. It could be in a church setting, with your spouse, your children, or those who called themselves friends. In this season, you are being tested to see if you will LOVE them unconditionally. The Lord will continue to put them in your face until you pass the test of unconditional love. On every end, you are showing how much of your flesh has died. Truth be told, it has nothing to do with how badly they have offended, hurt, or rejected you. It's all about whether or not you will allow the Lord to heal your heart, and demonstrate the same grace and love God gives you in great abundance every single day you rise. Look at the countless ways we have disappointed God with our sinfulness. Think about the times you told Him you would obey in a certain area, yet didn't. Think about the times you told Him you wouldn't go back to certain bondages, but you did. YET, He in His infinite love for you, FORGAVE you and allowed you to live on!

Will you choose to stay hurt? Will you continue to be offended and upset every time you see that person? Will you be angry every time you hear their name or when your mind recalls the situation? Will you continue to rehearse and discuss it with others when you are supposed to let it go? Will you GROW UP in the love of Christ and release the hurt and offense to the Lord? Will you mature and walk in the love of God even if they don't apologize or their behavior doesn't change? My mind quickly goes to the Emergency TV announcement that says, "This is a test. This is only a test." Then, it goes into next steps of where to proceed in case of an emergency. The sooner we recognize it's a test and are determined to pass it with flying colors, the sooner we will mature and achieve sweatless victory. That is not to say that we won't feel "some kind of way" when our flesh is tested, or that we won't be bothered. However, when we yield our will to His will, we will experience a great level of PEACE. This will also catapult us to greater realms in the Spirit. We have now shown God we can be trusted to walk in love, especially when we don't feel like it.

So, going back to the text. Joseph was now in the place where he could be a blessing to the very ones who hurt him, primarily because he postured himself in the presence of the Lord. He received the healing he needed from God. He then allowed his imprisonment to become his place of favor, grace, and anointing. While Joseph was in prison, he allowed the Lord to pour the oil and wine of healing into him. During those moments of being and feeling forgotten, Joseph received the salve of the Holy Spirit into his heart and spirit. Had Joseph not allowed God to deal with him, he would've been toxic, bitter, and ineffective. The last thing you need to be in this season is bitter and ineffective. Joseph (now 13 years later) sees his brothers and is aware of his father's poverty. Now, he's positioned to be a blessing and assist them. What's interesting is that in Genesis 42:7, Joseph recognized his brothers (the ones who hurt him and sold him into slavery), but they didn't recognize him. I'm about to insert a revelation right now. When God is about to promote you and bring you out, you will recognize the ones who served as your enemies, but they won't recognize the Spirit of God on you because you are now transformed. You are now healed, delivered, whole, and fully equipped to be the vessel God wants to use.

God also used Joseph to test and discern the hearts of his brothers by accusing them of being spies and stealing from him. It was only upon their departure that Joseph discovered the "deception" and missing cup on Benjamin's person. As a result of their discovery and remorse, Joseph's brothers begged and pleaded with him to allow them to take Benjamin's place in prison. What a change of events! Any other time, they would've been out for their own interests and selfish desires. Not this time. Tragedy had struck and the impending sorrow that would've embraced their father's heart was enough to cause them to make a change in their posture and behavior. They could ill afford to lose another brother. After Joseph's test and imprisoning them for three days, going back to see their father, and providing their people with food, they returned to Egypt with both Benjamin and their dad, Jacob. Talk about a family reunion. Joseph used his position as governor to be a blessing, but also to see where the heart of his brothers lied. When they first approached him, they bowed in desperation and humility. They even recalled the pain they had caused from their behavior concerning Joseph being sold into slavery. These were different men. They were repentant and humbled now. It's amazing what turn life takes to push you to God, or to explain it even further, what it takes to show that you've changed (especially to someone you've hurt or offended).

We can now be as Joseph—forgiving, loving, and kind. To go further, Joseph was in a position to be a blessing, despite his painful experience and past with his brothers. Now, looking at your situation of having to express forgiveness, are you willing to move on? Are you willing to release them of the pain they caused you so that you can experience the grace, mercy, and forgiveness God so freely shows you? This is your new opportunity for freedom, liberty, and peace. Ephesians 4:32 (KJV) says, "And be ye kind one to another, tenderhearted, forgiving one another, even as God for Christ's sake has forgiven you." Forgiveness isn't saying the guilty party is correct about how they treated you, but it is giving yourself freedom from the prison of pain they've caused in your heart and mind. It doesn't mean that you'll be best buddies with them, it just means you've relinquished penalizing or judging them for their wrongdoing. Nobody deserves the power and pain of hurtful wrath and rage. It is now time to move on to the better things God has in store for your life. You won't be fully effective in ministry if you hold on to the pain, abuse, mistreatment, bondage, betrayal, and rejection. The purpose of God is greater than that. Joseph embraced the opportunity, and proved through his affliction that his God had a purpose in all of his pain. Your pain has a purpose too. While letting it go is never easy, it is most definitely worth it!

CHAPTER 11

THE MANIFESTATION IS FINALLY HERE!

In the previous chapter, we discussed the blessing and power of letting go, forgiving, and moving on. That is just the catalyst to propel you into your manifestation.

My mind goes to pregnancy, and the blessing of childbirth. When I first married my children's dad, I immediately became pregnant with what I called a "honeymoon baby" and unfortunately miscarried that baby at nine weeks. That baby stopped developing and lost his heartbeat. Well, almost seven months to the date, I became pregnant with my son, Anthony Jr. While I was overjoyed at another opportunity to become pregnant and carry a child, it was not without its challenges. I had crazy morning sickness, and lost about 20 pounds. Then, I started cramping and experienced light bleeding, only to find out at 19 weeks that my cervix was softening (like butter) way too soon. As a result, I had a cerclage put in and went on bedrest until delivery. When it was finally time for Anthony to come, I was in labor (and I do mean LABOR) for 26 hours. This little fella didn't want to come quickly. My little pastor-prophet Anthony arrived on July 28, 2000, at 10:21 p.m., at the measly weight of six pounds, nine ounces.

However, when I got pregnant with Bethany, it was considerably easier (even though I did return to medical bedrest at 30-32 weeks, but no cerclage this time). Labor, however, was extremely painful but FAST. My water broke at 8:30 p.m. while watching *7th. Heaven*, and we arrived at Holy Cross Hospital at approximately 9:00 p.m. I got changed in the hospital bathroom and nearly pulled the red help cord out of the wall! The nurse escorted me back to the bed. I told her, "This baby is coming!" She didn't believe me until she checked me and saw that I was nine centimeters dilated. They told me she would be born in 30-45 minutes and they were right. My little Sweet Pea (as I so affectionately call her) was born July 8, 2002, at 10:41 p.m. and was seven pounds even! Talk about COMPLETION and PERFECTION! Interestingly enough, her name was always Bethany Jordan (totally Holy Spirit inspired) and the doctor that delivered her was named Dr. Lazarus. Isn't that funny? Anyway, the point of my pregnancies and births is multi-faceted. The first point was that pregnancy in and of itself for some women is very easy and they have no problems whatsoever. For other women, it's very difficult and some experience miscarriage, stillborn births, and in my case bedrest.

Even with successful pregnancies, there are difficulties, like my encounters with bedrest both times and a long first labor. Then, there's morning sickness, nausea, backaches, swollen ankles, mood swings, crazy appetites, labor, delivery, and recovery. Whew, that was a mouthful! The second point is, just as each pregnancy is different, your trial is custom made for the purpose and plan God has sketched out as the Master Architect of your life. He used that very situation and test to bring out the best in you. He used it to bring out the God in you! He wants and expects fruit from what you went through.

As I reflect on those moments of labor, you tend to think it is excruciatingly painful, and it seems as though it will never end. You just want the baby OUT already. You've prepared for it, you set up the baby registry, got your nursery theme, colors, and furniture. You've gone online and checked out baby names, what they mean, their origin, etc. Pregnancy can be the most exciting time in a woman's life, but the most fearful. You start wondering if you'll carry to term. Will the baby be healthy or deformed? What will labor be like? Will the baby be ugly? (I just had to throw that in there, because we do think about things like that.) Is the baby a boy or a girl? Will I have a C-section or vaginal birth? Will I need an epidural or will I make it without meds? Will I make it on time to the hospital or give birth on the side of the road? These, plus hundreds of other questions, can bombard your mind. You may feel the same way spiritually about that thing that you've experienced. How long will I be in this situation? When will I come out? Will I even make it out? Well, if you're reading this, you made it! You are now arriving at the finish line. You've got the victory well within your grasp. You are hoisting your 1st place ribbon, your Lombardi (Super Bowl) trophy is in your right hand!

I can't help but to go back to pregnancy and labor because it's such a powerful parable to serve as a point of reference. The roughest part of labor is the crowning stage, the part just before the baby's head comes out. In case you didn't know, there are roughly three stages of labor. There are the contractions, active labor, and pushing and delivery. You may just be in the beginning stages of labor—your test or trial, so it might not be so trying. You may also be starting to feel the intensity of your battle, so you may be in the active labor phase. In this active labor phase, it's like the heat has been turned up, but you can still handle it without missing a beat. As things get progressively worse, you will soon move into what is considered the pushing and delivery stage. That's the phase of your life when all hell breaks loose, and when you're hit with back to back trials, etc. You almost feel like you can't make it. You're doing everything in your power to make the pain stop. You are looking for every form of medical intervention possible. You're hunting for the epidural. You're physically exhausted. You're mentally exhausted. All you want to do is hold your baby. All you want to do is see your baby. You are ready to see that which you've carried for months.

Well, here it comes. The promise is now fulfilled. After that final push, it comes out. It comes forth in fullness. Let's take one final look at the Scriptures concerning Job's manifestation. Remember, Job had pretty much gone through hell and high-water between losing his children, his cattle, sheep, and home; even his body was physically afflicted with boils. He endured and suffered false accusations from his wife and friends. Enough is enough already! Just when you think you're done with one thing, you have to go battle something else. I'm not sure of the timeline of how long Job had to endure these issues, but one day (to me) was long enough! Scholars say it was roughly nine months. How prophetically interesting, since that's how long it takes to carry and give birth to a child. Understandably, throughout the book of Job, he expressed complaints and disdain for his misfortune.

Well, now, payday had come to Job's house! Sidebar: Ever notice how it's the TIGHTEST just before payday? Well, it was time for Job's BONUS CHECK! The Lord received Job's prayer of repentance and ultimate worship (Job 42:1-6). In response to Job, God spoke to his frenemies (friends who later acted as enemies): Eliphaz, Bildad, and Zophar, and commanded that they offer a sacrifice and allow Job to pray for them because they were wrong in what they said to Job. That's what God is going to do for you in this final season of affliction. He's going to cause your enemies or frenemies (whatever you may choose to call them right now) to bless you RIGHT IN FRONT OF YOUR FACE! The caveat is that you must pray and intercede for them. You must have your heart in such a loving and forgiving condition that it prepares the soil of their heart to be ready for your harvest.

Psalm 23:5 (NIV) says, "You prepare a table before me in the PRESENCE of MY ENEMIES." So, you will get to see your enemies BLESS YOU.

You will make one final push and out comes your manifestation. Out comes your promise. It was born out of great pain and labor. You were faithful during your test. You didn't give up, even when you felt all hope was lost. Your promise is here. You get to hold it in your arms and look at what the Lord has done!

David said in Psalm 119:71 (KJV), "It is good for me that I have been afflicted; that I might learn thy statutes." Trouble is what kept me close to God. The pain I experienced kept me learning the Word at His mouth. It kept you praising, praying, and seeking God's face! Even when I wanted to take off running, I learned to run to Him! You can now rejoice because you made it through. You made it out victoriously, without the smell of smoke in your hair or on your clothes. Yes, you even loved the very ones who said you wouldn't make it through. Though they hated on you and slandered your name, you held your head up, held your faith up, held your praise up, and kept on pushing through! You fought with the weapons God provided and gained the victory. You've made it through suicide attempts, bad decisions, bad relationships, poor choices, financial hardships, health issues, and then some! Now, it's your time to RECEIVE!

Your "Job Double Portion Blessing" is now hitting your house. I prophesy to everyone reading this book that because you took the time to intercede for your enemies, to love and forgive them, not only will God restore all you lost, but exceed your expectations. The blessing that the Lord is imparting is about to blow your mind in a way that has never been done before. It goes beyond finances and good health. It will propel you into your next place of destiny. It will help you accomplish God's purpose for your life. You are now equipped to handle warfare and greater things with considerable ease.

Let's recap: You didn't go through your situation for yourself. It was strategically and divinely orchestrated by God to accomplish His purpose and lead others closer to Christ. Had Job not endured financial and health challenges, and the loss of his children, he wouldn't have ever understood the divine will of God. He wouldn't have had a clue about the plan God had for him to intercede for his frenemies. The trials Job endured pushed him closer to the face of God and into an active pursuit of God's presence. It strengthened Job's trust in God.

It is my prayer that those who read this book will truly get that the pain of what you've experienced in this life is not about YOU, but about God's purpose FOR you! There are people God will now connect you to that will need the wisdom and guidance you received from your furnace of affliction.

Use this time to reflect on what you've learned, and as a result you will be a catalyst and point of reference for the goodness of God. The greatness God has imparted into you from this season has ignited wonderful gifts, talents, skills, and abilities you never knew existed.

Here is a final Scripture I want to leave with you:

Genesis 50:20 (KJV)—"But as for you, ye thought evil against me; but God meant it unto good, to bring to pass, as it is this day, to save much people alive."

The devil meant to take you out when it came to your tests, trials, afflictions, and tribulations, but as the Scripture just indicated, "God meant it unto ***GOOD, to bring to pass… TO SAVE MUCH PEOPLE ALIVE."***

I know the fire is hot, and it seems to be turned up seven times hotter than you can bear, but God has a purpose for all of it.

Go through with a praise and you will experience victory! You can say with an emphatic praise as King David of Israel said in Psalm 119:71 (KJV), hence the title of this God-breathed book, "It is good for me that I have been afflicted; that I might learn thy statutes."

If just one word of this book has encouraged you, feel free to pass it on, purchase it for a friend, and let others know that it is my heartfelt desire to see people healed, whole, saved, and free in the arms of Jesus Christ.

ABOUT THE AUTHOR

Jetaune Randall-Slaughter was born in Washington, D.C. She is the oldest of three sisters and is also blessed with two brothers. Although Jetaune has not obtained a college degree, she has been through "The School of Hard Knocks." Shortly after accepting Christ as a young teen and being filled with the Holy Spirit as a young adult, Jetaune discovered her spiritual gifts as an intercessor, exhorter, teacher, and prophet. She firmly believes in ministering truth in a loving and humorous manner, and her mission is to ensure that others know the value of an intimate and growing relationship with Jesus Christ.

Although living for Christ is Jetaune's biggest priority, she enjoys reading and writing, and is a die-hard Dallas Cowboys fan and an armchair NFL Analyst. Through her previous marriage, Jetaune was blessed with two wonderful children, Anthony and Bethany. In February 2014, she married the love of her life, Herbert Slaughter.

To connect, email Jetaune at jetaunerandallslaughter@yahoo.com

CREATING DISTINCTIVE BOOKS
WITH INTENTIONAL RESULTS

We're a collaborative group of creative masterminds with a mission to produce high-quality books to position you for monumental success in the marketplace.

Our professional team of writers, editors, designers, and marketing strategists work closely together to ensure that every detail of your book is a clear representation of the message in your writing.

Want to know more?
Write to us at info@publishyourgift.com
or call (888) 949-6228

Discover great books, exclusive offers, and more at
www.PublishYourGift.com

Connect with us on social media

@publishyourgift

www.ingramcontent.com/pod-product-compliance
Lightning Source LLC
Chambersburg PA
CBHW071528080526
44588CB00011B/1599